OPENING UP THE SOVIET ECONOMY

JERRY F. HOUGH

Opening Up the
Soviet Economy

Opening Up the Soviet Economy

JERRY F. HOUGH

THE BROOKINGS INSTITUTION
Washington, D.C.

Copyright © 1988 by

THE BROOKINGS INSTITUTION

1775 Massachusetts Avenue, N.W., Washington, D.C. 20036

Library of Congress Cataloging-in-Publication Data

Hough, Jerry F., 1935–
  Opening up the Soviet economy.

  Includes bibliographies and index.
    1. Soviet Union—Foreign economic relations.
2. Soviet Union—Foreign economic relations—United
States.   3. United States—Foreign economic relations—
Soviet Union.   4. Soviet Union—Economic policy—
1986–   . I. Title.

HF1557.H68 1988   338.947   87-36835
ISBN 0-8157-3747-5 (pbk.)

9 8 7 6 5 4 3 2 1

Set in Linotron Times Roman
Composed by Monotype Composition
Baltimore, Maryland
Printed by Jarboe Printing
Washington, D.C.

THE BROOKINGS INSTITUTION is an independent organization devoted to nonpartisan research, education, and publication in economics, government, foreign policy, and the social sciences generally. Its principal purposes are to aid in the development of sound public policies and to promote public understanding of issues of national importance.

The Institution was founded on December 8, 1927, to merge the activities of the Institute for Government Research, founded in 1916, the Institute of Economics, founded in 1922, and the Robert Brookings Graduate School of Economics and Government, founded in 1924.

The Board of Trustees is responsible for the general administration of the Institution, while the immediate direction of the policies, program, and staff is vested in the President, assisted by an advisory committee of the officers and staff. The by-laws of the Institution state: "It is the function of the Trustees to make possible the conduct of scientific research, and publication, under the most favorable conditions, and to safeguard the independence of the research staff in the pursuit of their studies and in the publication of the results of such studies. It is not a part of their function to determine, control, or influence the conduct of particular investigations or the conclusions reached."

The President bears final responsibility for the decision to publish a manuscript as a Brookings book. In reaching his judgment on the competence, accuracy, and objectivity of each study, the President is advised by the director of the appropriate research program and weighs the views of a panel of expert outside readers who report to him in confidence on the quality of the work. Publication of a work signifies that it is deemed a competent treatment worthy of public consideration but does not imply endorsement of conclusions or recommendations.

The Institution maintains its position of neutrality on issues of public policy in order to safeguard the intellectual freedom of the staff. Hence interpretations or conclusions in Brookings publications should be understood to be solely those of the authors and should not be attributed to the Institution, to its trustees, officers, or other staff members, or to the organizations that support its research.

Foreword

OVER the last few years we have seen one development after another in the Soviet Union that would have been unthinkable at the beginning of the decade. American and British politicians critical of the Soviet Union appear uncensored on Soviet television; American inspectors will be able to visit sensitive Soviet defense sites; and western investment will be encouraged in the Soviet Union, with western managers supervising Soviet workers.

In this study Jerry Hough argues that these are signs of a fundamental change in the Soviet Union. The isolation of Soviet society has turned out to have a fatal flaw: the near-total protection for Soviet industry has produced the same adverse economic consequences that it would in other countries. If the Soviet Union is to remain a great power, it must dramatically open up its economy and its society and subject its industry to foreign competition.

The purpose of Hough's study is to explore Mikhail Gorbachev's foreign economic strategy and its implications for Soviet domestic politics and foreign policy. But since any such basic change in the Soviet Union poses fundamentally new choices for the United States, Hough examines these as well—both the choices of American businessmen as they decide whether to invest in the Soviet Union and the choices for American society as it grapples with how to structure the relationship between the two superpowers.

Jerry F. Hough, an associated staff member at Brookings, is James B. Duke professor of political science and public policy studies at Duke University and director of its Center on East-West Trade, Investment, and Communications. He would like to thank Peter Hauslohner, Ed A. Hewett, and John D. Steinbruner for their helpful comments on the manuscript. He would also like to thank the many Soviet scholars and officials who over the years have been willing to discuss important issues with him, and especially Georgii Skorov of the Institute for the Study of the USA and Canada, who arranged useful interviews in 1986. Ruth Blau and Caroline Lalire edited the manuscript; Mark R. Thibault and Amy Waychoff verified its factual content.

The project was financed by the Carnegie Corporation of New York, the John D. and Catherine T. MacArthur Foundation, and the Andrew W. Mellon Foundation. Brookings is grateful for that support.

The views expressed here are those of the author and should not be ascribed to the persons or foundations whose assistance is acknowledged above, or to the trustees, officers, or other staff members of the Brookings Institution.

BRUCE K. MACLAURY
President

December 1987
Washington, D.C.

Contents

ix

1

Introduction

THE United States has for years been concerned about possible Soviet attempts to split the NATO alliance. The conclusion of an agreement on intermediate- and short-range missiles in Europe (the zero option) has increased fears that General Secretary Mikhail S. Gorbachev pushed for the withdrawal of American missiles in order to "decouple" Europe militarily from the United States. This view represents a fundamental misperception of the forces behind Soviet policy.

Although Gorbachev has accepted a zero option that Leonid Brezhnev would not accept, it would be wrong to conclude that his goal is the decoupling of the United States from the defense of Europe. He has repeatedly denied that he wants to break up the NATO alliance, and he is sincere. The Soviet Union needs NATO as a justification for maintaining Soviet troops in Eastern Europe. It fears that a breakup of NATO would eventually lead West Germany to acquire nuclear weapons in order to achieve equality with Great Britain and France. A high Soviet official gave another reason privately in September 1987 when he was asked why the Soviet Union wanted to preserve NATO: "We do not want a united Germany."[1]

The explanation for Gorbachev's willingness to accept the zero option lies outside the military sphere. Brezhnev desperately wanted to stave off reform, but Gorbachev has

1. In this instance and throughout the book, Soviet officials have been quoted in private, off-the-record conversations with the author or in his presence.

passionately embraced "radical reform," which he equates with a "new revolution."[2] In fact, it was this change from an anti-reform policy to a pro-reform one that was to produce the change in Soviet policy toward European missiles.

It is the purpose of this book to explain why and to explore the foreign policy implications of economic reform. In August 1985 Gorbachev deliberately closed an interview with *Time* magazine with the statement that "foreign policy is a continuation of domestic policy." He said that the Soviet Union had "grandiose" domestic plans and raised the question, what international conditions do they require? But he ended the interview with an ambiguous response: "I leave the answer to that question with you."[3] I will try to provide it, focusing on two major issues.

First, how does foreign policy fit into Gorbachev's strategy for overcoming resistance to reform? Does an arms control agreement, coupled with a summit meeting with the American president, strengthen his authority and his ability to force through reform? Or does Gorbachev need a foreign threat and a symbol of the dangers of Soviet technological backwardness such as the Strategic Defense Initiative (SDI) to justify the sacrifices that reform will require? Second, what are the foreign policy imperatives of reform from an economic point of view?

Everybody takes for granted the closed character of the Soviet economic system. The Soviet Union has permitted no foreign investment; it has imported goods only through a monopolistic ministry of foreign trade; it has not permitted its factory managers to enter the world economy independently with their exports or even given them an incentive system that encourages exports. Although these measures are not usually considered "protectionist," the word is appropriate, and protectionist policies are as disastrous for

2. *Pravda,* August 2, 1986, and September 20, 1986.
3. "Special Report: Moscow's Vigorous Leader," *Time,* September 9, 1985, p. 29.

economic performance in the East as in the West. Ultimately they will have to be dismantled if reform is to succeed.

When western observers look at Soviet economic problems, they correctly say that the first and in many ways easier path to progress is through the introduction of competition at home. They see any significant attack on protectionism coming at a later stage of reform. A high Soviet banking official made the same point privately when he said, "We need a convertible ruble at home before we can have a convertible ruble abroad."

This analysis is correct from an economic point of view. The Soviet reintegration into the world economy will not have a major effect on Soviet gross national product over the next few years. But the analysis is, I think, incorrect from a foreign policy point of view.

In the first place, the Soviet Union has no need to dichotomize its policy and introduce domestic and foreign competition in sequence. The relatively unreformed economy of East Germany has performed far better technologically than other socialist economies, and the access of East Germany to the European Community is surely one explanation. Even without a radical domestic reform, the pressure on Soviet plants to increase exports will subject them to foreign competition abroad and force them to improve the quality of their production. Already, a Soviet economist reports privately, the Vladimir Tractor plant, which now exports 50 percent of it product, turns out better goods for the home market than before. Surely the Soviet leaders will be trying to create the same pressure on the rest of Soviet industry as quickly as possible.

In the second place, the actual change in foreign policy will be a gradual process, for the Soviet Union has contradictory requirements. It will not receive large-scale foreign investment or engender a more relaxed attitude toward technological control unless it adopts a less threatening military posture. Yet it is more persuasive for Gorbachev to tell the Soviet people that increases in meat prices and in the possibility of unemployment are necessary for defense than to tell them that these policies are required in order to reduce the time wives spend on shopping. Using the defense argument at home while reducing the sense of threat abroad obviously poses a subtle problem.

Similarly, the Soviet Union must undermine any American technological blockade if it is to reintegrate its economy into the world economy. This means a more forthcoming policy toward Europe, Japan, and the industrializing third world countries, but that will not be easy without undermining the western military alliances that the Soviet Union wants to maintain.

These contradictory purposes are well served by a treaty with the United States to remove missiles from Europe, confirmed at an abbreviated summit that reaffirms the dangers of SDI. As time goes on, however, Soviet foreign policy change will become more sweeping. In July 1987 Eduard Shevardnadze spoke bluntly to a group of Soviet diplomats:

> The time has come . . . . to "economize" our foreign policy, if such an expression is permissible, since, until it is linked wholly with the economy, it will be unable to help in restructuring our domestic economy and society. . . . We should become a more organic part of the world economic system, and we can and are obliged to become so if we accept and assimilate the forms extant in it.[4]

The foreign policy requisities of economic reform will be in place long before the reform itself succeeds or fails, and the United States will have to respond.

Our first problem is to understand what is going on. The Soviet Union will be permitting the kind of foreign investment and seeking the types of foreign economic cooperation that

4. *Vestnik ministerstva inostrannykh del SSSR,* no. 3 (September 10, 1987), in Foreign Broadcast Information Service, *Daily Report: Soviet Union,* November 3, 1987, p. 89.

we have in the past considered unthinkable. But because they were unthinkable, we literally have not thought about them. During the first two years of Gorbachev's regime, we have tried to deny the reality of change instead of considering how to respond to it. If we do not come to understand Gorbachev's overall strategy—if, for example, we continue to confuse an effort to break the American technological blockade with an effort to break up NATO—we will continue to make mistake after mistake in our policy.

Our second problem will be to respond to a much broader sweep of Soviet policy. We will have to decide whether the reform of Soviet domestic and foreign policy is in our interest, whether to try to encourage or retard it, and the best means to do so. We will have to assess the strength of our position, the extent to which we do or do not have the power to affect Gorbachev's options, and the extent to which we can put explicit or implicit conditions upon our cooperation.

2

The Context of Reform

A SOVIET general secretary who wants to implement a major reform faces a fundamental dilemma. Reform must be incremental, or the result will be economic chaos. Yet the economy is so interconnected that reform in one sphere may well fail without simultaneous and comprehensive changes in other spheres. In addition, if economic reform is gradual, opponents have a long time to sabotage it. A general secretary's central concern must be how to sequence the various steps of reform in a way that solves this predicament. To understand what Mikhail Gorbachev is doing, one must understand the economic and political logic of a successful reform. The first step in that direction is to understand the economic and political context in which Gorbachev is operating.

The Economic Context

Gorbachev should be quite familiar with the nature of Soviet economic problems, as well as their most basic causes.[1] These issues have been extensively discussed in the Soviet press for thirty years, and they must be doubly familiar to any person who served as regional party secretary for as long as Gorbachev did. Furthermore, he has promoted some of the best economists in the country to high positions, and they

1. For a discussion of the problems, see Joseph S. Berliner, *The Innovation Decision in Soviet Industry* (MIT Press, 1986), and Ed A. Hewett, *Reforming the Soviet Economy: Equality versus Efficiency* (Brookings, 1988).

6

can assist him if there are subtleties and interconnections in the system that he does not understand.

The basic problem with the Soviet economy is that, with the exception of the private plot in agriculture and the illegal "second economy" in the services, it has been completely "owned" by the state, with each branch of the economy administered by a monopolistic ministry. No one has been permitted to establish an independent store, an independent restaurant, or an independent factory to fill some societal need.

Moreover, within the state sector, managerial officials work in a planning and incentive system that discourages innovation, economizing of material and labor, and high-quality production. Enterprise plans are quite detailed. They specify the number of workers, the amount of supplies (with the actual suppliers specified), the amount and nature of capital investment, and so forth. Output plans are dictated by the supply plans. If a manager's suppliers are included in the plan, the same must be true of the names of his customers and the items that must be produced for them.

Managers are judged on a number of plan indicators, but the crucial fact is that the indicators have been set at the beginning of the year and specify concrete outputs and inputs. In a real sense, supplies and workers are cost-free to the manager as long as they are included in his plan. In Gorbachev's words, "In practice, any expenditures are covered [and] sales of production are essentially guaranteed."[2] Thus the planning system itself institutionalizes a seller's market, and the results are predictable. Even if managers desired to do so, they are not free to change suppliers; consequently, they are not in a position to object decisively if the supplies they receive are not top quality.

Managers do receive bonuses if they overfulfill their plans. However, there are disincentives to increasing their sales

2. *Pravda*, June 26, 1987.

drastically or economizing on labor, for the new levels would simply be fixed as the base for next year's plan, which would then be more difficult to fulfill. Officials around the world know what happens if they return appropriated funds at the end of the budget year. Fortunately for Soviet managers, the temptation will never be strong to overfill the plan substantially, for they could not get the needed additional supplies if they wanted. Higher organs try to overcome these incentives to be conservative—and, of course, the quantity and quality of Soviet production has increased over the years—but the quiet managerial resistance has a pervasive impact.

The economic system produces another, perhaps even more fundamental, problem: the plans are much too detailed simply to be imposed from the top, for the central organs do not have enough time and knowledge to do the job for the entire economy. Hence plans must be compiled much like budgets in the West. Lower officials present draft plans in which they say what they need and what they expect to produce. Higher organs—the ministries and the State Planning Committee (Gosplan)—have the job of balancing the requests for workers and supplies with the available labor force and with other output proposals. The correct western analogy to have in mind is the requisition process by which lower military units or large bureaucratic organizations get supplies.

There are several serious consequences of this system, as in the budgetary processes of any bureaucracy. First, requests for innovative products must rise through a system of committees and scientific-technical questions, through a whole series of review processes. Radical ideas can thus be easily sidetracked or defeated. In addition, because new chemicals, new electronic parts, new consumer fads, and the like often have a very short period before they are superseded by something else, the lengthy decisionmaking process can mean that the product will be obsolete before it comes out. Western chemical companies often do not propose producing advanced specialty chemicals in the Soviet Union because they will have become outmoded or will have evolved into cheap mass products before they finally can come on line.

Second, even if the decision process could be expedited, managers have little incentive to make innovative proposals or to propose economizing measures. Because performance is judged by the fulfillment or the nonfulfillment of a fixed plan, intelligent managers are always seeking an easy plan. They propose as low an output plan as they can and try to avoid complicated goods that may be difficult to produce, let alone new products, which almost always have bugs at the beginning. They have even less of an incentive to suggest a lower level of supplies or a smaller work force for their plants. The result is that continuously expanding demand is built into the system. Again, Gorbachev is crystal clear on the essential problem: "The very system of obtaining supplies is precisely what creates shortages."[3]

Third, the planning system creates virtually total protection from foreign competition for Soviet manufacturers. Since supplies are "free" for the manager, the planning process ensures that requests for raw materials and capital goods always exceed supplies. Consequently, no domestic manufacturer need lose any business to foreign goods imported for the use of industry. Indeed, the regime even deliberately tries to restrict imports to goods that are not produced in the Soviet Union, but even if they did not, the infinite demand for capital goods would prevent any real competition. Furthermore, so long as Soviet manufacturers have a totally captive domestic market, they have no incentive to export products where they would face both variable demand and an insistence on high-quality, innovative production.

Compare the position of the Soviet manufacturer with that

3. Ibid.

of the Japanese. While entry of foreign goods into the Japanese market is severely restricted, local businessmen must compete with those that do enter the country. Foreign companies create plants inside Japan that compete with local manufacturers. Although Americans talk about a trade deficit with Japan, this is true only in balance of payments terms. The value of goods produced by American firms inside Japan and goods imported from the United States roughly equals the sum of Japanese goods exported to America and those produced by Japanese firms inside the United States.[4] In addition, domestic Japanese manufacturers are interested in the exportation of their goods, and sometimes the government prods them in this direction. Thus they must compete with western manufacturers in foreign markets, and such competition is doubly difficult because it involves satisfying foreign tastes. Although we often talk about Japanese protectionism, in comparison the Soviet Union makes Japan look like an open economy.

Western economists have had great difficulty grasping this problem,[5] for they use the word *protectionism* for practices such as tariffs and quotas employed by governments to protect industries from the natural working of the market. Because the Soviet Union does not have a market economy or even a convertible currency, foreign trade is not regulated

4. In 1984 Japan imported $25.6 billion worth of goods from the United States, and $43.9 billion worth were produced by American firms located in Japan, for a total of $69.5 billion. Japan exported $56.8 billion worth of goods to the United States, and $12.8 billion worth were produced by Japanese firms in the United States, for a total of $69.6 billion. Kenichi Ohmae, "Japan's Trade Failure," *Wall Street Journal,* April 1, 1987.

5. There have been important exceptions. For example, see Edward A. Hewett, "Most-Favored Nation Treatment in Trade under Central Planning," *Slavic Review,* vol. 37 (March 1978), pp. 25–39; and Franklyn D. Holzman, *Foreign Trade under Central Planning* (Harvard University Press, 1974), pp. 139–63.

through tariffs and the like, but is conducted through direct negotiations. Because the Soviet Union does not use traditional techniques of protectionism, it is not seen as protectionist.

Yet in the 1920s Lenin posed the issue explicitly in "infant industry" terms. In 1921, when he introduced the New Economic Policy (NEP), which allowed private agriculture and a private sector in services and small-scale light industry, a number of high-level officials pushed for an NEP in foreign economic relations as well. They wanted to accept a compromise offered by David Lloyd George at the 1922 International Economic Conference in Genoa in which the Soviet Union would recognize its prewar foreign debts in exchange for a restructuring of the debts that would put them within the Soviet capability to pay. They also wanted to abolish the state monopoly of foreign trade and to implement such decentralized forms of protectionism as tariffs.

Lenin's rejection of the advice to recognize the foreign debt was almost hysterical,[6] and in discussing a letter by Nikolai Bukharin, one of the proponents of a lessening of the power of the foreign trade ministry, Lenin directly called for a protectionism that went beyond tariffs:

> Our border is maintained not so much by customs or border guards as by the monopoly of foreign trade. This Bukharin does not see—and this is his most striking mistake . . . that no tariff policy can be effective in the epoch of imperialism and of the monstrous difference between poor countries and incredibly wealthy ones. Bukharin several times refers to tariff protection, not seeing that any of the rich industrial countries can completely break this protection. . . . Russia can be made an industrial power not by any tariff policy, but exclusively by a monopoly of foreign trade. Any other protectionism is in Russia's contemporary condition completely

6. A. O. Chubar'ian, *V. I. Lenin i formirovanie sovetskoi vneshnei politiki* (Moscow: Nauka, 1972), pp. 261–82, especially pp. 272–73.

fictitious—a paper protectionism. . . . We should struggle against this with all our might.[7]

Lenin's last great battle was a vigorous and successful effort to reverse his subordinates' policy.[8] Lenin's policy was continued by his successors, but was really institutionalized and strengthened not by the monopoly of foreign trade, but by the planning system that was established in the 1930s.

With the exception of the problems of protectionism, all of the difficulties of the Soviet economy and the nature of possible solutions have been widely discussed for years. Enterprise managers should be judged by a profit indicator rather than by a fixed output plan, and should pay for their supplies and labor out of their proceeds from sales rather than having inputs allocated to them.[9] They should have greater independence from the ministries and Gosplan so that they can respond quickly to changing consumer demand. They should be free to change suppliers so that the fear of losing business will force the suppliers to keep the quality of their production high. And, of course, since their own customers will be free to change suppliers, managers must keep production innovative and of high quality so that they themselves do not lose business. Finally, they should receive big rewards if they take risks and are successful, for otherwise

7. V. I. Lenin, "O monopolii vneshnei torgovli," in V. I. Lenin, *Polnoe sobranie sochinenii* (Moscow: Politizdat, 1964), vol. 45, pp. 334–36.

8. See the discussion in Richard B. Day, *Leon Trotsky and the Politics of Economic Isolation* (Cambridge: Cambridge University Press, 1973), pp. 73–76, and V. S. Pozdniakov, *Gosudarstvennaia monopoliia vneshnei torgovli v SSSR* (Moscow: Mezhdunarodnye otnosheniia, 1969), pp. 26–35.

9. Gorbachev is very clear about this and made an analogy to NEP: "Let's pay for resources out of profit. For labor resources, for supplies, for water, for land. . . . Pay for resources—that was the idea of the food tax [in NEP]. They gave you a hectare, they gave you two—you paid for each hectare, but everything else was yours." *Pravda*, June 13, 1987.

they fall prey to incentives to keep profits growing slowly and steadily rather than to maximize them.

All of this is easy to say, and many Americans have the feeling that only ideological blindness or bureaucratic resistance stands in the way of reform. In reality, the situation is far more complex than that. Reform in the Soviet Union is technically very difficult. The various parts of the economic system are closely interconnected, and partial changes must be done carefully lest they are nullified by other aspects of the system. If, for example, managers were simply given greater independence and were free to change prices, they could easily maximize profits by raising prices unless other enterprises were free to enter their markets to take advantage of the improving profit margins. None of this "freedom" would have any real meaning, however, without the additional freedom to change suppliers and to find new suppliers to meet increased demand. The question then arises: how are all these changes compatible with planning?

Reform is also politically difficult. The existing Soviet price system does not correspond to the supply and demand equilibrium point, and irrationalities often are not the result of random factors, but of deliberate social policy. For decades the leadership has attempted to promote a more egalitarian distribution of income, and it has done far more than limit the gap between the wages of workers and those of managers. For example, it has prohibited private services and trade in large part because of a fear that they would create a relatively wealthy group of traders, and has heavily subsidized the prices of many of the basics of life so that they will be affordable to everyone. These include utilities, mass transportation, medical care, college education, cultural attractions, housing, and food, especially bread and meat. (The state pays four rubles, eighty kopecks for a kilogram of meat and sells it for one ruble, eighty kopecks.)[10] Preserving a

10. Interview with Abel Aganbegian, Prague Television Service,

planning system that encourages excess demand for labor is part of the same social policy, for everyone understands that this makes unemployment impossible.

Any serious economic reform in the Soviet Union, therefore, must go well beyond a lessening of ministerial power. It must also involve a fundamental change in social policy. Income distribution must become less egalitarian to provide greater incentives; prices must be brought into line with the forces of supply and demand, which means substantial increases in the prices of sensitive goods such as meat and bread; incentives must be given to economize on labor, which means at least temporary unemployment must be implemented; and Soviet industry must be subjected to the sting of foreign competition, eliminating the factors in the existing system that have protected workers as well as managers. Foreign investment inside the Soviet Union will mean either that some workers will feel exploited by foreign managers or that they will be paid enough extra to make other workers feel cheated. All the Soviet talk about discipline, in traditional American terms, really means "an increase in managerial prerogatives." In short, major economic reform in the Soviet Union will have some of the characteristics of the social policies of Reaganism and Thatcherism.

The Political Context

Simply listing the imperatives of economic reform gives the reader a sense of many of the political obstacles to reform. First, if economic reform must attack the heart of workers' benefits, workers cannot be expected to be enthusiastic. When the Polish government took the first steps toward reform by raising meat prices, workers rioted. Soviet leaders have to fear that the same thing might happen in the Soviet

July 1, 1987, in Foreign Broadcast Information Service, *Daily Report: Soviet Union,* July 10, 1987, p. R19.

Union, and they know that workers' riots are enormously dangerous in communist systems. The educated middle class is not as supportive of the system, and if workers were to become deeply dissatisfied, other groups might quickly join the fray. The refusal of Russian soldiers to fire on those demonstrating against food shortages brought down the tsar in 1917, and this memory must haunt the Soviet leaders today.

Ministerial and Gosplan officials will also scarcely favor a major reduction in their power and a major change in the way that they must conduct their jobs. Enterprise officials may like the idea of increased power, but they are production engineers who are used to a seller's market. They cannot look forward to an economy in which they must become market-oriented and in which the customer is king.

Anyone who has followed the American press in recent years knows that westerners have emphasized the strength of this bureaucratic resistance. The Central Committee's removal of Nikita S. Khrushchev in 1964 and the selection of a cautious party bureaucrat as his successor led Zbigniew Brzezinski to speak of "a government of clerks" and of "oligarchic petrification" in the mid-1960s: "The ruling bureaucracy, I fear, will oppose any efforts to loosen the grip of the party on Soviet society and to increase the range of social autonomy. . . . It is for [this] reason that I lean toward the stagnation-degeneration pattern."[11]

While Brzezinski focused on the consequences of men with a bureaucratic mentality becoming party leaders, other analysts increasingly began to emphasize the impact of the bureaucracy itself. The conventional explanation for the failure of the gradual reforms of the 1960s was bureaucratic

11. Zbigniew Brzezinski, "Victory of the Clerks: What Khrushchev's Ouster Means," *New Republic,* November 14, 1986, pp. 15–18; *Between Two Ages: America's Role in the Technetronic Era* (Viking Press, 1970), p. 165; and "Concluding Reflections," in Z. Brzezinski, ed., *Dilemmas of Change in Soviet Politics* (Columbia University Press, 1969), p. 153.

resistance, and the prevailing western analysis of the stag-
nation of the late Brezhnev period focused on systemic
factors. Although the old theories of totalitarianism emphasized the enormous strength of the general secretary, the new
interpretation insisted that the Soviet leader was a weak
political superstructure, controlled by the bureaucratic "ruling class." This view became dominant in the 1970s, and was
encapsulated in more popular writings in the title of Michael
Voslensky's book, *Nomenklatura: The New Soviet Ruling
Class* .[12]

In recent years western analysts have also emphasized
other political obstacles to reform besides bureaucratic and
worker resistance. The political culture and the ideology,
which used to be said to damn "trade-union consciousness"
and to support sacrifice of the present for the future, now are
said not only to oppose the "immorality" of the market but
also to be conservative bulwarks of privilege and comfort.
The Russian people, who once were described as messianic
and anarchic and who conducted two of the great revolutions
of this century in 1905 and 1917, are now supposed to meekly
accept all indignities and demands emanating from the authorities. The Communist revolution, which formerly was
seen as an unnatural departure from Russia's path to consti-
tutional democracy, now is simply an insignificant blip in a
Russian historical tradition featured by inevitable repression
and xenophobia.

Finally, western analysts emphasize presumed Soviet
fears that reform would lead to loss of control of Eastern
Europe and the non-Russian republics in the Soviet Union.
Liberalization in the mid-1950s and the mid-1960s was followed by the Hungarian revolt in 1956 and the Prague Spring
in 1968. Recent events in Poland are seen as evidence that
Eastern Europe is ready to explode if there is any loosening
of the controls.[13] And, of course, any Soviet Marxist who

12. Michael S. Voslensky, *Nomenklatura: The New Soviet Ruling
Class,* trans. Eric Mosbacher (Doubleday, 1984).

13. This factor is emphasized in Seweryn Bialer, *The Soviet*

thinks that political power and economic power are linked may believe that economic decentralization to the republics will soon result in political decentralization as well.

Yet in focusing so much on the political obstacles to reform in the Soviet Union, western analysts have fallen into a one-sided analysis of the Soviet political scene. Although it would be foolish for a general secretary or for us to ignore these obstacles, it would be just as foolish to assume that they are the sum total of the political context in which Gorbachev operates.

Even a listing of the obstacles to reform reminds us that there must be ambivalences and countervailing forces. If reform means a reduction of worker privilege and an increase in managerial power, then clearly many bureaucrats have a powerful reason to support reform as well as to oppose it. Russians may fear a decentralization of power to the republics, but non-Russians, who constitute nearly 50 percent of the population, should favor it—and may become restive without it. If ideologues fear the "injustices" associated with the market, they should find the immorality associated with the illegal black market (the second economy) even more distasteful, and they may favor legalization as the best practical option. And if the Soviet Union fears that it will suffer the same consequence of price reform as Poland, so should other Eastern Europeans. The Hungarian evolutionary path in the 1970s led to a better life, while the Polish revolutionary path led to martial law and an economic depression. Eastern Europeans may be quite willing to give reform a chance over the coming five to ten years.

The political pressure for reform, however, goes far beyond the sum of these partial types of group support. There are two major political facts that, in my opinion, outweigh all others. First, a fundamental change has been occurring in the composition of the Soviet population, and in a direction that

Paradox: External Expansion, Internal Decline (Knopf, 1986), pp. 204–10.

is supportive of reform. Second, the legitimacy of the old system—and it had considerable legitimacy—rested on its claim that it contributed to the defense of Russia and an increase of its national power. Now it is clear that the old system increasingly has had a negative impact on the achievement of those goals.

The change that has occurred in the Soviet population is both sociological and psychological. The Russian Empire at the beginning of the century was a rural society at the early stages of industrialization. At such a time the largest number of ambitious and talented upwardly mobile members of society are going from the peasantry into skilled and unskilled blue-collar jobs in the city, and the number of such jobs rises rapidly. Workers thus became an important political force in the West in the early decades of industrialization, and they were even more important in Russia.

At later stages of industrialization, the proportion of blue-collar workers, first of unskilled and then of skilled ones, begins to decline, and the mass movement of the ambitious and talented in society is from blue-collar jobs into managerial and professional ones.[14] Political measures that are conducive to stability and support from the most politically relevant stratum at one stage have the opposite effect as the demographic character of society changes. The Soviet Union has reached the point of diminishing political returns from a policy that grants privileges to blue-collar workers, especially privileges that permit them to work without discipline.

The psychology of the Soviet people has also undergone a major change. One reason is the transformation of the population from illiterate or semiliterate into one in which the young now normally have a high-school diploma and an increasingly large percentage have some college education.

14. For a table showing the structural upward mobility in the Soviet Union from 1939 to 1970, see Jerry F. Hough and Merle Fainsod, *How the Soviet Union Is Governed* (Harvard University Press, 1979), pp. 564–65.

In 1965, 30.6 million Soviet citizens had high-school diplomas and 5.6 million college degrees; in 1986 these figures had increased to an estimated 117 million and 20.1 million, respectively.[15] A second reason is the movement of a large proportion of the population from small farming villages of a few hundred people to cities with over 100,000 people (40 percent of the population now live in the latter).[16] For all the differences between democracy and dictatorship, between capitalism and socialism, the lives of today's youth in a large Soviet city are far closer to the lives of the young in a large American city than to that of their great-grandparents in a rural Russian village.

A more subtle—and perhaps more important—psychological change has also taken place. Those who developed the totalitarian model were correct when they said that left-wing extremist movements such as communism and right-wing extremist movements such as Nazism (or Khomeinism, to use a contemporary example) have more similarities than differences. Both left-wing and right-wing extremism are essentially nativist rejections of modern western society.[17]

Scholars like Adam Ulam have noted that Marxist revolutions were occurring only in the early stages of industrialization,[18] while Walt W. Rostow called communism "a disease of the transition."[19] If Rostow had had the more recent experiences of Afghanistan, Angola, Ethiopia, Nicaragua,

15. Tsentral'noe statisticheskoe upravlenie pri Sovete Ministrov SSSR, *Narodnoe khoziaistvo SSSR v 1964 g.: statisticheskii ezhegodnik* (Moscow: Statistika, 1965), p. 33 (hereafter *Narkhoz*); and *Narkhoz 1985*, p. 27.

16. Calculated from *Narkhoz 1985*, pp. 5 and 18–23.

17. See Hannah Arendt, *The Origins of Totalitarianism* (Harcourt Brace, 1951).

18. Adam B. Ulam, "The Historical Role of Marxism and the Soviet System," *World Politics*, vol. 8 (October 1955), pp. 20–45.

19. Walt W. Rostow, *The Stages of Economic Growth* (Cambridge: Cambridge University Press, 1960), p. 162.

and Yemen before him, he might have added "and the pre-transition."

Ulam's and Rostow's insights are crucial to an understanding of the Soviet system. The people who supported the Bolshevik revolution—and the Bolsheviks had a majority of the vote in the cities and the central agricultural regions whose peasants worked part-time in the city—were people of the transition in the truest sense of the phrase. Like the rural inhabitants of Iran streaming into the cities in the 1960s and 1970s, they were frightened by the strange ways and values of the city, which they associated with the West. Whatever Lenin may have had in mind while he was in self-exile in Western Europe, those who received his message inside Russia sensed that his program meant a course of development for Russia that rejected the economic and political institutions of the West, its contemporary values, and, most clearly of all, the westernized elite that Peter the Great had created inside Russia itself.

The essence of the system that was set up under Lenin and especially Stalin was to destroy the power of the westernized people and to establish two iron curtains—one against strange, unsettling, even satanic western ideas, the other against unsettling market forces, especially foreign ones. Stalin represented, if in extreme form, the hatred of the West and of alien classes that produced the revolution in 1917.

Those who were between the ages of forty and sixty in the 1950s and 1960s—one might call people of this age the "ruling generation"—were the insecure youth of the transition in the first quarter of the twentieth century who then identified themselves with the transformation of 1928–1932. They were the equivalent of the teenagers of Teheran of the 1970s. By the mid-1950s they had lost any revolutionary fervor they once may have had, but they retained their earlier insecurities and their earlier fears of market forces and new western cultural developments such as rock-and-roll. In 1959 the British observer Edward Crankshaw called these people of the Brezhnev generation "the lost generation":

The flower were killed in the great purges or in the war; what remains, with exceptions, are the survivors—who survived either because they were too stupid to be considered dangerous, or because they brought sycophancy to a fine art, or because they were as cunning as the fox. Nothing in this world is more depressing to contemplate than the average Soviet official of high or low degree at present between the ages of forty and sixty [i.e., born between 1900 and 1920]. And, as would be expected, those who started their rise in their thirties during the great purges of twenty years ago . . . are incomparably the worst.[20]

By 1985 the situation had changed fundamentally. The generation that had been content with the changes of the 1950s and wanted to consolidate them with Brezhnev was passing from the political scene. The people in their fifties in the 1980s—the "ruling generation"—were a post-transition generation. They took industrialization for granted, and associated it with victory in World War II. When they were young, they did not show any deep fear and hatred of western culture, but instead were enormously attracted to everything western: blue jeans, jazz, films, books, rock-and-roll, the chance to travel abroad.

Edward Crankshaw, whose 1959 views of the Brezhnev generation were negative, had a different opinion of those beginning to rise into the elite at the time:

The Soviet Union's great hope lies in the young—those under thirty-five [that is, born after 1924]. The best of these, and there are many who are very good by any standards, inhabit a world of their own which has every appearance of being utterly different from the world of their elders. . . . In a dozen professions in which Party control is particularly rigid—in the Foreign Service, in the Law, in journalism, in economics, in radio, in the higher civil service with its many branches, in the armed forces, in the university faculties, you will meet

20. Edward Crankshaw, *Khrushchev's Russia* (Baltimore: Penguin Books, 1959), p. 91. I am grateful to Professor Sheila Fitzpatrick of the University of Texas for this reference.

well-turned-out young men in their thirties, usually Party members, relaxed and easy in manner, often with a pleasantly ironical approach to life, and very much in touch with realities of every kind. . . . These confident and unfrightened young men are springing up like grass. . . . I have been talking of the cream of the younger men beginning to rise in what are called the liberal professions and the State and Party service. Until the last decade young men of comparable ability would not have dreamt of this sort of career.[21]

Many factors have led to this situation. Gorbachev's generation was ten years old when the war started, and many remember high-school teachers who had been trained before the revolution. The Americans were allies during their formative years, and the xenophobia of their late teens only gave the West a forbidden-fruit quality. But paradoxically Stalin himself made a crucial decision that undercut his own xenophobia. By placing a heavy emphasis on classical Russian literature as a part of the school curriculum, he indoctrinated the youth in the western-oriented values of the nineteenth-century Russian intellectuals. Indeed, because the works of the Slavophile conservatives were generally suppressed, the youth were disproportionately exposed to the westernizing stream in the literature.

The twenty-year-olds of the 1950s are now the fifty-year-olds of the 1980s. They no longer want blue jeans, but their personal interests still center on a freer press, on greater access to western culture, on greater freedom to travel abroad, and, of course, on a better selection of goods and services in the domestic economy—in short, precisely on those things that could be expected to be the consequence of reform. In addition, as Wolfgang Leonhard has pointed out, bureaucrats are always dependent on superiors, and real security can be provided only by property. This gives them a vital interest in a private sector.[22]

21. Ibid., pp. 127, 130.
22. Wolfgang Leonhard, *The Kremlin and the West: A Realistic Approach,* trans. Houchang E. Chehabi (Norton, 1986), p. 160.

Further, one should not underestimate the nostalgia of fifty-year-olds for the great events of their youth. The great events for the Gorbachev generation were the de-Staliniza-tion of the Twentieth Party Congress in 1956, the poetry readings on daring themes that attracted thousands of young people, the World Youth Festival in Moscow that brought tens of thousands of foreign youths to Moscow for the first time in decades, the breaking of one taboo after another in culture and in the writing of history, and the promise of technological superiority that was symbolized by the Soviet Union's being the first to launch a satellite and then a man into space. The young who were inspired by Khrushchev's appeals at that time are now between forty and sixty. They remember the unrealized promises and are not satisfied with the more modest changes that have actually taken place. The impact of the bureaucrats' personal interests on their political attitudes is diluted by their occupational interests, but by the same token their personal interests also introduce great ambivalence into the bureaucratic resistance to reform.

The workers too have become different from what they were earlier in the century. Even in the more advanced Russian republic, 92.9 percent of the workers in 1939 had left school before even entering high school. By 1970, 20.2 percent of all Soviet workers had a high-school diploma, and by 1979, 41.7 percent.[23] This dramatic increase in educational levels in the 1970s obviously reflected changes among the young. It is symptomatic that in 1959, 28.1 percent of army draftees had left school before high school, 47.4 percent had entered secondary school but dropped out, and only 24.5

---

23. Calculated from Tsentral'noe statisticheskoe upravlenie pri Sovete Ministrov, *Itogi vsesoiuznoi perepisi naseleniia 1959 goda: RSFSR* (Moscow: Gosstatizdat, 1963), pp. 278, 280, 293, and 295. In these calculations, agricultural workers and peasants were subtracted from those listed as being in physical—as opposed to "mental"—work. Tsentral'noe statisticheskoe upravlenie SSSR, *Chislennost' i sostav naseleniia SSSR: Po dannym Vsesoiuznoi perepisi naseleniia 1979 goda* (Moscow: Finansy i statistika, 1984), p. 157.

percent had a secondary degree. By 1986, 97 percent were high-school graduates and the other 3 percent high-school dropouts.[24]

These bare figures represent many changes in attitude. Workers, perhaps even more than intellectuals, have favored rock-and-roll, and they seem equally attracted to western films and mass culture. Moreover, workers who are high-school graduates are increasingly middle class in psychology. A top Soviet economist privately reports that workers don't like the wages of the foreman to be so low, for they want the possibility of rising to that higher-status post. The ambitious among them must look upon the privatization of services as yet another avenue of upward mobility for themselves.

Sociological change alone would not, of course, overcome inertia, but events changed the amount of political ammunition in the hands of supporters and opponents of the status quo. By 1965 it was still possible to think that the Soviet system, improved with minor adjustments and helped by the importation of western technology, could move forward rapidly and become the model for at the least the third world. Leonid Brezhnev had been the Central Committee secretary in charge of the military and the defense industry from 1956 to 1960 when the first Sputniks were launched, and hence he symbolized the great technological advances made by the Soviet Union. Egypt, Indonesia, and Burma were only the most prominent of the countries that gave indications of following Fidel Castro's path to the left. The United States had not yet landed a man on the moon, and Japan was only beginning its economic surge toward world primacy.

By 1985, however, the Soviet Union was falling behind such countries as South Korea in its ability to export manufactured goods to the West, and Japan was becoming the model for both the third world and other countries. President Reagan's espousal of the Strategic Defense Initiative and the

24. *Kommunist vooruzhennykh sil*, no. 10 (May 1987), p. 79.

suddenness of the American breakthrough on superconductors symbolized the Soviet fear that technological backwardness was dangerous for defense in the long run. The modernization of China raised the specter that a country with a billion people and territorial pretensions on the Soviet Union might follow the path of other Asian countries to industrial dynamism.

As a consequence, the social forces in the Soviet Union that pushed for reform, including an opening to the West, had become much larger and better placed in the mid-1980s than they had been in the mid-1960s, let alone in the mid-1950s. In addition, they could now plausibly say that reform was indispensable. They could say that Russia would not remain a great power and that the Soviet system would not remain stable unless the Soviet Union raised its technology to world levels, and they could say that an opening to the West was necessary for that end. Like Gorbachev in June 1987, they could say that Russia was in a pre-crisis (*predkrizisnyi*) situation.[25] When people's views of what should be correspond with their views of what must be, pressure for action becomes enormous. A general secretary who will be only sixty-nine years old in the year 2000 and who will like to usher in the new century in triumph has every reason to adopt their arguments.

In my judgment, the ubiquitous talk about meaningful conservative opposition has been grossly overdone. This opposition has been decisively and conclusively defeated. Gorbachev's real political problem comes from the opposite direction. Industrialization seriously erodes the legitimacy of right-wing dictators, and communist reformism in Hungary, Czechoslovakia, and Poland also got out of hand. There is every reason to think that industrialization produces powerful liberalizing forces in the Soviet Union as well. The meaningful opposition to Gorbachev will come from the

25. *Pravda*, June 26, 1987.

intelligentsia, and the control of that opposition is his primary political problem. When in October 1987 the Moscow party boss, Boris Yel'tsin, decided to stake out a position more liberal than Gorbachev's, he was betting that the liberal social forces were so strong that eventually the party would have to turn to someone who could accommodate them.

3

The Strategy of Reform

DESPITE Mikhail Gorbachev's bold language about economic reform, relatively little such reform occurred in his first year and a half in office. Many Soviet intellectuals and western observers pointed to the obstacles outlined in the previous chapter as the reason for the difference between words and deeds. Then in the winter of 1986–87, the regime ratified a series of potentially quite radical decisions that legalized private labor, independent cooperatives, and joint ventures based on foreign investment. Most analysts still insisted that political opposition would prevent these measures from being carried out to any significant degree. The June 1987 plenum of the Central Committee, with its decision on economic reform and its three additions to the Politburo, temporarily stilled this talk of major opposition, but talk of defeats and opposition recurred in the fall.

Possibly the dire predictions for Gorbachev will prove to be correct, but, as noted earlier, a policy-relevant analysis must begin at another point. Since Gorbachev told the editors of *Time* that "foreign policy is a continuation of domestic policy,"[1] it is important to understand the steps that he has taken in his first years. Many western analysts assumed that he was learning on the job and improvising. This may be true of minor steps, but the evidence strongly suggests that he has had a general strategy of reform—and a general foreign policy strategy to go with it. A failure to grasp this strategy risks serious foreign mistakes on the part of the West.

1. "Special Report: Moscow's Vigorous Leader," *Time,* September 9, 1985, p. 29.

Consolidation of Political Power

Gorbachev faces many tasks in reforming the Soviet Union, but the most immediate has been to maintain majority support in the Central Committee. The Central Committee not only can veto any reform but is also the institution with the power to elect and dismiss the general secretary and the Politburo members. This fact requires that the general secretary be very careful in dealing with the Central Committee, but if he controls the Central Committee he has real independence vis-à-vis the Politburo.

In 1985 Gorbachev had a ticklish political problem with the Central Committee. It had been elected in 1981 and was composed of the top 300 officials in office toward the end of the Brezhnev era. Most members of the Central Committee clearly understood that change was necessary, or they would not have elected a young man with Gorbachev's ideas.[2] Nevertheless, it was one thing to support reform in general and another to be enthusiastic about specific important reforms, and Gorbachev needed a Central Committee more beholden to him personally and more committed to reform. In addition, new and younger officials would normally be more energetic as administrators.

Thus it was in Gorbachev's interest to remove as many as possible of the old officials on the Central Committee from their jobs in the government or party apparatus before the Twenty-seventh Party Congress in February 1986 so that their replacements could be elected to the Central Committee at that time. This, however, created a dilemma and a danger.

2. John Crystal, an Iowa banker with whom I talked in the spring of 1987, visited Gorbachev in his Central Committee office in 1981. Unlike most Soviet offices, normally furnished in a stodgy, old-fashioned way, Gorbachev's was tastefully decorated with modern Scandinavian furniture. Gorbachev was telling all the officials who visited him that he was a modern man and would modernize—really Europeanize—Russia if he was elected.

A person stays on the Central Committee until the new election at the conclusion of the next party congress, even if he is retired or demoted. The more Central Committee members Gorbachev removed, the more might be inclined to vote against him because of personal grievances. In fact, by February 1986, 38 percent of the living, voting members of the Central Committee had been retired or seriously demoted—a very large bloc of the members.[3]

Gorbachev's solution to this dilemma was to be cautious with policy innovation until a new Central Committee was elected. In foreign policy he changed no personnel other than Andrei Gromyko himself until the eve of the party congress, no doubt for fear of antagonizing the former foreign minister. By speaking a good deal about change but doing little, Gorbachev created enough uncertainty to prevent anyone from organizing against him.

In the long run Gorbachev had to put together a solid working majority in the Central Committee that would support real reform. Of those who make up the Central Committee, the central government ministers and chairmen of state committees, as well as the deputy chairmen of the Council of Ministers who supervise them, have the most to lose in a reform and can generally be expected to oppose it. They constituted 22 percent of the 319 voting members elected in 1981 and 18 percent of the 307 voting members elected in 1986.

A reforming general secretary can mobilize a variety of different types of Central Committee members to overcome the opposition of the central government officials. Seven percent of the voting members of the Central Committee elected in 1986 were military officers, and many of them had to be concerned about the impact of Soviet industrial defects on Soviet weaponry; 5 percent of the voting members worked

3. The calculations in this chapter are based on my compilation of leadership changes as reported in the Soviet press.

in the Ministry of Foreign Affairs, and many of them must have been concerned with the impact of economic defects on the world standing of the Soviet Union; 8 percent were workers and peasants, and they may have had a natural inclination to follow a vigorous general secretary who was attacking higher bureaucrats.

Nevertheless, if a general secretary wants to attack the power of the central government machinery, he has no hope without gaining the support of the provincial party and government officials. They constitute 38 percent of the voting members of the Central Committee, and if they combine forces with the central government officials, they can block any action.

Fortunately for a reforming general secretary, the regional officials are his natural base of support. Historically the general secretary's first job has been supervision of the party apparatus, and he has an important role in the selection of its officials. This has always been a key factor in his consolidation of power, for the provincial party secretaries have been in control of the regional delegations to the party congresses. If the general secretary controls the regional party officials, he gains effective control of the party congresses and of the Central Committee they elect. In fact, throughout Soviet history, provincial officials have normally supported the general secretary in his struggles against his enemies in the party leadership. (The exception in 1964 came two years after Nikita Khrushchev offended the regional party secretaries by splitting the regional apparatus into separate rural and industrial units.)

Moreover, regional party officials have relatively little influence on the directives and plans of the ministries that shape the life of the region and are usually angry at the ministries and at Gosplan for neglecting local interests. They have far more power over provincial governments and local enterprises, and a decentralization of power to the local or enterprise level would increase local party influence as well.

If reform placed greater emphasis on individual taxation and left this money more at the disposal of local governments, the provincial party secretaries would approve.

Hence the first step for any reforming general secretary must be to consolidate his support among the provincial party secretaries, and by all indications Gorbachev devoted a great deal of attention to this. From 1978 to 1983 Gorbachev was the Central Committee secretary for agriculture, which gave him intimate contact with the provincial secretaries. He seems to have developed good relations with the younger ones, and may have had an important role in selecting them. Of the twenty-eight regional first secretaries in the Russian republic at the time of Leonid Brezhnev's death who had been born after 1925, twenty-five were in the same or a higher post in 1986 at the time of the Twenty-seventh Party Congress, and one of the others had died. Given the large-scale turnover among all other types of officials, Gorbachev must have thought that he could count on these younger men.

When Yurii Andropov became general secretary, he quickly gave the responsibility for personnel selection to Gorbachev, who began changing regional first secretaries rapidly. He continued this process after he himself was elected general secretary. At the time of the Twenty-seventh Party Congress in 1986, 26 percent of the provincial first secretaries were the post-1925 men who had been elected in the Brezhnev period, 26 percent had been named to their posts during the Andropov-Chernenko period when Gorbachev had been the personnel secretary, and 32 percent had been elected afterwards. Over 60 percent of Congress delegates came from regions with post-Brezhnev secretaries.[4]

4. The stenographic reports of the proceedings of the party congresses include the names of all delegates, together with the party organization that they represent. Through tedious effort, one can count the number of delegates selected in each party organization that elects them: the regions (*oblasti*) in the large republics, the small republics, and the cities of Moscow and Kiev.

The provincial first secretaries who were elected while Gorbachev was personnel secretary or general secretary had very different backgrounds from the provincial first secretaries of the Brezhnev period. The latter had almost all been promoted from within the region, a personnel policy that symbolized Brezhnev's willingness not to challenge his lower officials. Under Gorbachev, the new first secretaries have normally either been sent to the region from another region, or were local officials who had worked for some time in the Central Committee apparatus—often as an inspector of the Central Committee. Thus Gorbachev had a chance to know them personally, to judge their capabilities, and to assure himself of their personal loyalty. These men were the heart of Gorbachev's political machine.

After the party congress, Gorbachev continued consolidating his support within the regional party apparatus. Between March 1986 and October 1987, new first secretaries were named in 39 of the country's 149 regions, 41 percent of the regions headed by a secretary selected before Gorbachev became general secretary. In December 1986 the leader of the second largest republic, Kazakhstan, was replaced with a Great Russian, Gennadii Kolbin, who had been second secretary in Georgia on Stavropol's border when Gorbachev was first secretary there. Two months later the Belorussian party leader was made a Central Committee secretary, handling economic questions, which created another crucial job opening in the regional apparatus. A relatively minor party official with an agricultural background was promoted to this post over the heads of senior officials; he certainly seems to have owed his job to the general secretary. During 1987 the Ukrainian organization also came more under Gorbachev's control: between March and August, seven of the twenty-five regional party organizations received new first secretaries, and a new party leader was appointed in the independent capital, Kiev, as well.

At the Central Committee plenum in January 1987, Gorbachev talked a good deal about "democratization." Gorbachev also advocated the election of enterprise managers, and this principle was actually incorporated into the draft of a new enterprise law that was published a week after the plenum.[5] He also said that "some comrades" had proposed the secret ballot election of regional party secretaries, but this proposal was not endorsed in the resolution passed at the end of the plenum.

One can well understand why "some comrades" would like the election of regional party secretaries. Such a step would gut the power of the general secretary, and for this reason it is unlikely that Gorbachev would support any such change that had real meaning. Similarly, the election of factory managers by workers would not be a good strategy for a general secretary who wants to strengthen managerial discipline over workers, to increase wage inegalitarianism, and to divert money into investment. If these elections of managers are typical Soviet elections, however, they have one enormous political benefit for Gorbachev. They take the power of appointment of managers from the ministries and give it to provincial party officials, who will "organize" the elections. This would increase the power of Gorbachev's machine and its happiness with its boss. Boris Yel'tsin apparently wanted to push democratization further, but Gorbachev dealt with his challenge in a summary fashion.

Gorbachev built his support on the regional party officials in another way. At the end of the Brezhnev era, the members of the Politburo and Secretariat located in Moscow had (with the exception of Gorbachev) worked in high posts in Moscow for over twenty-five years on the average. They had worked in the same job for thirteen years. Andropov's and Gorbachev's policy was to bring people from outside Moscow into the Politburo and Secretariat. This not only ensured that holders of key central posts would have a fresh perspective

5. *Pravda*, January 28, 1987.

but also strengthened the general secretary's political support in the provinces.

Gorbachev used his great strength in the Central Committee and party apparatus to change radically the composition of the Politburo and the Secretariat in his first years in office. The Politburo contained ten voting members after Konstantin Chernenko's death—nine in addition to Gorbachev himself. Three of these nine were removed in 1985, a fourth (Dinmukhamed Kunaev) in 1986, and a fifth (Geidar Aliev) in October 1987, while a sixth (Gromyko) was moved to a ceremonial post. Eight new voting members were added to the Politburo by October 1987. Moreover, at this date, four of the six candidate members of the Politburo had reached candidate status after Chernenko's death, as had nine of the ten Central Committee secretaries beneath the level of Gorbachev and Yegor Ligachev. It was an unprecedented performance.

When Gorbachev added new members to the Politburo, he was able to select men who had been much inferior to himself in status in November 1982 when Brezhnev died. At that time Gorbachev had been a Politburo member for three years and had made an alliance with Andropov in which the latter became the general secretary and Gorbachev the personnel secretary and heir apparent. Except for his close friend, Eduard Shevardnadze (the minister of foreign affairs), his new colleagues on the Politburo were on a much lower level then. Ligachev (the second secretary) was a first secretary in remote and small Tomsk province; Nikolai Ryzhkov (the chairman of the Council of Ministers) was one of four first deputy chairmen of Gosplan; Nikolai Sliun'kov (the Central Committee secretary for economic coordination and construction) was a deputy chairman of Gosplan—even lower; Lev Zaikov (the Central Committee secretary for the military, the defense industry, and machinebuilding) was chairman of the executive committee on the Leningrad city soviet—the seventh or eighth ranking job in the city; Viktor Chebrikov (the chairman of the Committee for State Security, or KGB) was a first deputy chairman of the KGB, a post that never has been a stepping stone upward; Aleksandr Yakovlev (the Central Committee secretary for ideology and foreign policy) was ambassador to Canada; Viktor Nikonov, the Politburo member for agriculture, had been a deputy minister of agriculture. Even in March 1985, when Chernenko died, not one of these men was a full member of the Politburo. Gorbachev not only removed five 1984 Politburo members but did not promote a single one of the other members to a higher post.

One can always advance different interpretations of Kremlin politics, but by far the most plausible explanation is that Gorbachev selected his inner core of top lieutenants from men of small stature in 1982—men who at that time surely had no expectation of ever being Politburo members—precisely because they would see themselves on a quite different level from Gorbachev. And the fact that he did not promote a single member of the old Politburo strongly suggests that he did not have to cut any deals within the Politburo to get himself elected, that real power resided in the Central Committee, and that there he already had an extremely strong position.

During the winter of 1986–87 rumors about major political opposition to Gorbachev swirled through Moscow, the result of deliberate leaks. The second secretary, Ligachev, was said to be a conservative rallying point against Gorbachev. The Ukrainian party leader, Vladimir Shcherbitsky, was rumored to be an opponent whom Gorbachev had unsuccessfully tried to remove.[6] Some reports said that Gorbachev had only two sure votes on the Politburo, and some scholars thought that he might have only a year or two in office.

It was all highly dubious. Informally Soviet officials have always tried to depict the general secretary as an embattled supporter of détente with the West and a better life inside the

6. Philip Taubman, "Gorbachev Push to Win Control in Ukraine Seen," *New York Times,* March 22, 1987.

Soviet Union. (In 1948 President Truman believed such rumors about Stalin and actually said publicly that old Joe is "a decent fellow, but he's a prisoner of the Politburo. He would make certain agreements . . . but they won't let him keep them.")[7] Whatever Gorbachev's position in the Politburo, that body is not the ultimate center of power in the Soviet Union, and the pattern of events suggested that Gorbachev was extremely strong in the ruling Central Committee.

Consider what happened from December 1986 through April 1987, when Gorbachev supposedly was being defeated. As already noted, he replaced the first secretaries of Kazakhstan and Belorussia and took the power of appointing plant managers away from the industrial ministries. He promoted his top strategist, Aleksandr Yakovlev, into the Politburo and removed the conservative Central Committee secretary who had been keeping *glasnost* out of history discussions. He named a fellow student from Moscow State University (Anatolii Luk'ianov) as Central Committee secretary in direct charge of the secret police and the military. He appointed a man from his native province of Stavropol as chairman of the investigatory People's Control Committee, and in June he talked about giving it control of all inspections in the system. In the Ukraine in March and April, he changed the first secretaries of five of twenty-six regional party organizations, including two from Shcherbitsky's home province of Dnepropetrovsk. (The rumors about Shcherbitsky did not reflect a defeat for Gorbachev, but the first signal that the attack on Shcherbitsky was beginning.) And these were the months when the laws on individual labor, cooperatives, and joint ventures were passed, when Aleksandr Sakharov was released, and when the Central Committee approved a party conference that almost surely would be able to introduce changes in the Central Committee membership itself in 1988.

7. *New York Times*, June 12, 1948.

When a foreign plane penetrated to Red Square at the end of May, Gorbachev dismissed the defense minister and the head of air defense in summary fashion.

In my opinion, by the spring of 1987 Gorbachev was in as strong a political position as Stalin had been in 1927 or 1928.[8] In June 1987 he dramatized his strength further by having three Central Committee secretaries—Viktor Nikonov, Nikolai Sliun'kov, and Aleksandr Yakovlev—made full members of the Politburo. Not only did all three seem close to Gorbachev personally, but their selection meant that seven of fourteen Politburo members were full-time employees of the Central Committee apparatus that Gorbachev headed—seven of thirteen after Geidar Aliev was removed in October. To use an American analogy, the Politburo had come to be dominated by White House staff at the expense of the government officials. Gorbachev himself was one of only four Politburo members who had been selected before Chernenko's death, and the position of most of the others seemed shaky.

This did not mean that Gorbachev had surrounded himself with yes-men who agreed with him on every question. Even an absolute dictator, had he any intelligence, would not make that mistake; Stalin certainly did not. At the end of his life Stalin had three top lieutenants: Lavrentii Beriia, the secret police chief, who seems to have been as reactionary as advertised; Nikita Khrushchev, the Central Committee secretary for personnel; and Georgii Malenkov, the Central Committee secretary for the state apparatus and foreign policy. Khrushchev and Malenkov, who shared the post of second secretary—and in that sense were Ligachevs of their day—were far more reformist than Stalin (and they were to change his policy from the first week after his death), but that only meant that Stalin was a sophisticated dictator, not an

8. For opposing interpretations, see the discussion in David K. Shipler, "Gorbachev's Style Veils His Substance," *New York Times,* November 1, 1987.

endangered one. A leader with advisers both to the right and left of himself plays them off against each other, keeping the morale of each high by giving all of them periodic victories. This, however, does not mean that he is in danger of being overthrown or that his basic strategy or policy line is in danger of being overturned.

Political Strategy

Ultimately any really substantial reform in the Soviet Union depends primarily not on a general secretary's consolidation of power within the Politburo and the Central Committee, but rather on his ability to persuade officials to work with a sense of enthusiasm and professionalism. He must persuade students and young intellectuals not to go into the streets in a large-scale and threatening way, and he must persuade workers not to riot in the face of higher prices, greater discipline, and demands for other sacrifices. He must accomplish this with respect to both Russians and non-Russians, whose interests and demands can be quite contradictory.

This is a complicated task, and politicians handle complicated tasks with varying degrees of skill. As Eduard Gierek demonstrated in Poland (and in another way Alexander Dubček in Czechoslovakia), communist leaders are just as capable as noncommunists of misreading a situation and taking decisions that lead to disaster for themselves. Or they can be placed in situations in which they do not have the ability to control the forces they are trying to lead.

Part of western analysts' judgment about Gorbachev's chances for success must rest on their assessment of his skills as a politician. Politics is a bit of a shell game in which a skilled leader focuses the attention of the major groups in society on those goals or alleged goals of the leader that each favors, while he distracts them from the consequences of his policy that each finds distasteful. It involves adopting a political strategy that does not arouse overwhelming opposition at any one time and that maintains a solid but shifting majority behind each policy step as it is announced in sequence.

Gorbachev has been observed in a number of political settings both at home and abroad, and he has never failed to impress. Despite being the youngest Politburo member, he adroitly maneuvered himself to the top and quickly moved aside his chief rivals. It is evident that Gorbachev has given a great deal of thought to what would constitute the best political strategy to overcome opposition and to achieve what he wants.

Knowing that Gorbachev has a political strategy and understanding it are, however, two different things. Gorbachev has a knowledge of the Soviet political system that no foreigner can match, and unless western observers understand the structure of power and group interests within which he is operating, they will totally misjudge the situation. The West certainly cannot take all his words as gospel, for one aspect of a successful political strategy consists of keeping the long-range political strategy ambiguous or even misunderstood. President Ronald Reagan, for example, never announced that a severe recession early in his administration was part of the solution to inflation.

Some of Gorbachev's political strategy is fairly apparent. First, as noted, he was extremely cautious in his policy decisions before the Twenty-seventh Party Congress elected a new Central Committee, and he correctly concentrated on changes in personnel. He emphasized such conservative themes as discipline, higher investment, and an attack on alcoholism. His innovative themes ("restructuring" and "activization of the human factor") were ambiguous enough in their language to cause no alarm. Indeed, most western observers concluded in 1985 that Gorbachev was not a serious reformer, and Soviet conservatives cannot have been certain that he was.

Second, when Gorbachev began to modify ideology, he did it in ways that tried to reassure conservatives. Just before he announced his radical proposals of June 1987, he savagely attacked an economist by name for suggesting that unemployment was needed.[9] He said almost nothing about the "market" and explicitly denied that any return to capitalism was involved. By June 1987, with Gorbachev looking on and not objecting as he did with other speakers, Oleg Bogomolov, the director of the Soviet Union's major institute on socialist countries, could rightly complain:

> In the reconstruction of the economic mechanism . . . there is one key question which, it seems to me, we rather shamefully avoid. This is the question of the market under socialism—naturally a regulated one. We speak about goods-for-money relationships, about wholesale trade, but we largely mention the word "market" in a negative context. And a market-man (*rynochnik*) is generally a cuss word.
>
> In general, according to Marx, if we speak about the production of goods and goods-for-money relationships, then it goes without saying that the cost of a good and the demand for it is determined not in Gosplan or in some other organs, but at the point when the consumer votes with his ruble.[10]

In his speech to the Central Committee plenum two weeks later, Gorbachev did talk about goods-for-money relations and "their skillful use through prices and financial-credit levers, the planned mastery and management of the market taking its laws into account," but again he largely avoided the explosive word.[11]

Nevertheless, Gorbachev began the process of redefining socialist property to emphasize cooperatives instead of state ownership and became increasingly emphatic. He often quoted Marx (who was in himself a code word for an opening to the West, for he was hated by the xenophobes as a German Jew who has exerted the greatest western influence on Russia).

9. *Pravda,* June 22, 1987.
10. *Pravda,* June 13, 1987.
11. *Pravda,* June 26, 1987.

Marx's language about a withering away of the state under communism, while vague, certainly does not suggest monopolistic state ministries running industry. When Gorbachev quoted Lenin, he often did so from speeches of the last years of Lenin's life, when the latter was defending the mixed economy of the New Economic Policy (NEP). The Soviet media began explicitly to endorse the NEP as Lenin's version of socialism, and in November 1987 Gorbachev spoke of Lenin's "cooperative socialism," while rehabilitating Nikolai Bukharin's ideas. He denounced Leon Trotsky viciously and then defined Trotsky's program as basically the program of the conservatives of the 1980s.[12]

A third clear element of Gorbachev's political strategy was that he associated his reforms with patriotism or nationalism. The communist revolution had always had strong antiwestern roots—a rejection of Peter the Great's westernized elite and of Western European institutions and the West's path of development—and those wanting autarky had wrapped themselves in the national banner. During the Civil War Lenin used foreign intervention to rally Russian support behind his regime, and then in the 1920s and the 1930s Stalin did the same with his slogan of "socialism in one country" and his impassioned 1931 appeal that Russia catch up in ten years or be destroyed. After World War II the victory against the Nazis was repeatedly used as a major source of legitimization for the party.

Gorbachev explicitly appealed to this tradition. He paid homage to the shock workers—the Stakhanovites—of the 1930s and emphasized the sacrifices in World War II on the fortieth anniversary of victory in 1985. He donated 50,000 rubles of foreign royalties to the construction of a monument to the soldier in the most beloved World War II poem, Vasilii Terkin.[13] From his first days in office, Gorbachev linked the

12. *Pravda,* November 3, 1987.
13. Tass International Service, July 1, 1987, in Foreign Broadcast Information Service, *Daily Report: Soviet Union,* July 8, 1987, p. R7. (Hereafter *FBIS-SU.*)

survival of the system and the fate of the nation to "restructuring," insisting that it was indispensable if Russia was to
remain a major power in the next century. He repeatedly
came back to this theme in one way or another.

In addition, Gorbachev was skillful in the way he handled
the varieties of nationalism in the multi-ethnic Soviet state.
In practice, a decentralizing economic reform that allowed
more play for market forces would benefit the non-Russian
nationalities. The private sector could begin to produce
goods, sell food, build restaurants, and so forth that satisfied
local national tastes, and real *glasnost* would permit a culture
and a writing of history that was more in tune with local
national moods. Politically, therefore, it was the Russians
who needed to be reassured, and to that end Gorbachev
reduced the representation of non-Russians on the Politburo.
Of thirteen voting Politburo members in November 1987, ten
were Russians. Under Brezhnev, the first secretaries of five
non-Russian republics were full or candidate members of the
Politburo, but only one was in November 1987.

When Gorbachev's appointment of a Russian to head the
party organization in Kazakhstan in December 1986 produced
riots, the Soviet newspapers gave the riots unprecedented
coverage. It was a sophisticated decision. Non-Russians saw
that such resistance would be crushed. The virtually simultaneous removal of the general secretary in China after riots
in Beijing reminded them that unrest might accomplish nothing more than the destruction of a reform that was in their
national interest. Moreover, liberal Russian intellectuals and
students, who might have been tempted to press for greater
reforms, were reminded that real democratization would give
a level of power to nationalist forces in the non-Russian
republics that few Russians wanted. Although many western
analysts assumed that the multinational character of the
Soviet Union might make stability difficult to maintain at a
time of reform, paradoxically it was precisely this multinational character that cooled the passions of the radicals of all

nationalities and gave Gorbachev real hope that he might keep the pressures for more rapid change under control.

A fourth aspect of Gorbachev's early political strategy was to speak incessantly about technological modernization, but to emphasize political changes (summarized in the word *glasnost,* or openness) instead of economic reform in his actual policy. Censorship of the media and cultural works became less strict. Rather radical criticism of the status quo and proposals for change were permitted to appear in the mass media. Then in January 1987 a plenary session of the Central Committee was devoted to the subject of "democratization," a word that implied greater participation and even some use of electoral mechanisms. In particular, factory managers were to be elected instead of appointed by the ministries. A party conference dedicated to "democratization" was promised for 1988.

It is possible only to guess why the policy of *glasnost* became meaningful before economic reform did. One obvious reason is that it makes sense to open up criticism of economic problems before introducing actual reform. *Glasnost,* however, went far beyond discussion of economic difficulties. It included an hour-long press conference with British Prime Minister Margaret Thatcher on Soviet television, the announcement of the publication of *Doctor Zhivago* and other previously forbidden novels, the release of a film that dealt very critically with Stalinism, and a gradual movement toward discussion of historical figures such as Trotsky and Bukharin.

It is likely that the timing of political reform was meant to serve a broader strategic purpose. As has been seen, the middle class—the bureaucracy—was ambivalent about reform. Most of it had to be uneasy about the effect of reform on its work life, but approved the Reagan-Thatcher-like social policy and the opening to the West. The early talk about discipline, alcoholism, and higher investment was not a promise of Stalinism, but of a social policy favored by the middle class. The political reforms were a promise of an opening to the West and a freer (but not totally free) life at home. *Glasnost* was real, but democratization was far more limited—and was the issue in the removal of Boris Yel'tsin.

The deal being offered the bureaucracy was symbolized by the publication of the law on joint ventures with foreign firms on the very day that the Central Committee plenum on democratization opened in 1987.[14] The reward for submission to the sting of foreign competition was a looser political system and an opening to the West. Indeed, managers engaged in foreign trade and joint ventures would be the ones with the greatest right to travel abroad. But there were also implicit threats. The removal of the ministries' right to appoint plant managers was a real show of strength vis-à-vis the top bureaucrats, and it was a warning of the dangers of opposition. The bureaucrats had to know that if they succeeded in sabotaging the economic reforms, the price would surely be the loss of the political reforms as well.

A fifth aspect of Gorbachev's strategy was to identify himself completely, almost foolhardily, with the cause of reform. Even in his first year, Gorbachev made extravagant promises about raising Soviet technology to world levels, and then in 1986 he began talking about radical reform and even revolution. He explicitly stated that the Soviet Union must be bold, must take risks. If he proved to be indecisive, if his reforms proved to be ineffective, then disillusionment would be unnecessarily severe, precisely because expectations had deliberately been raised so high. Gorbachev recognized this situation and explicitly took responsibility on himself.

Yet this strategy had major compensations. Essentially Gorbachev had deliberately painted himself into a corner. He had turned the question of reform into a vote of confidence on himself. Opponents knew that if they defeated reform, they would have to remove a popular general secretary, and

14. *Pravda,* January 27, 1987.

they knew that such an attempt was an extraordinarily risky strategy precisely because expectations had been raised so high. Moreover, Gorbachev would fight for his life if he was challenged, and opponents knew that as well. They had to ask themselves whether they could win in a test of strength, and Gorbachev's consolidation of power had to raise the gravest doubts about the answer to that question.

Gorbachev himself, but even more frequently his agents, upped the ante by talking about opposition. Sometimes information (in my opinion, often disinformation) was leaked about Politburo opposition; more often, people talked about generalized opposition in the bureaucracy and elsewhere. This talk had the effect of giving Gorbachev and his reforms a precarious appearance. Although I believe this appearance was a false one, it turned normal foot-dragging into political opposition to the general secretary and, therefore, was potentially very dangerous. It suggested to dissidents or reformers who would like to push Gorbachev further by going into the street (as students had in Beijing) that this would simply give Gorbachev's enemies an excuse to overthrow him and reverse the reforms. And if the reformers decided to do so anyway, Boris Yel'tsin's fate was a warning.

Through these various steps, Gorbachev almost surely bought himself five to ten years to see if the reforms that he wanted to introduce in the Soviet Union would pay off. If there were major riots or demonstrations that proved hard to control, then he might be sacrificed, but he had moved skillfully to forestall such riots beforehand. He benefited enormously from the fact that the country yearned for strong, capable leadership after a decade in which its leaders had been pathetically ill, and he gave every sign that he had the ability to lead strongly and capably.

Economic Strategy

The biggest obstacle to radical economic reform in the Soviet Union is not political or bureaucratic opposition, but the immense inherent difficulty of achieving the goals of reform itself. The West has not achieved the combination of steady economic growth, rapid technological development, and near-absence of unemployment that Gorbachev is seeking, and Yugoslavia's effort to move toward market socialism has been far from a success. There was, as Andropov and Gorbachev both rightly said, no magic "recipe" that would introduce the desired competition and flexibility into the system without producing chaos in the process.

Ultimately the economic and political strategies of reform had to be integrated. Economic reform could not be introduced all at once not only for political but also for technical economic reasons. It had to be phased in gradually, step by step. Even the easiest of the reforms—privatization of a substantial part of the services sector—required an almost unimaginable array of decisions about business licenses, the setting of optimal tax rates, rules of business operation, definitions of business expenses for taxation purposes, safety standards and nondiscrimination rules, consumer protection measures, the establishment of a reliable supply system, and so forth. Gorbachev had to reassure prospective participants who "are literate [and] remember, visibly, the fate of the 'Nepmen' [of the 1920s] and also that later, after the liquidation of the industrial cooperatives, some people had to go far from home."[15] Even if Gorbachev had total power, total commitment, and no opposition, it would take years to work out these questions alone.

The general secretary had many things to consider as he decided on the sequence of steps to be taken, and he himself was explicit about some of them: "It is impossible to move forward successfully by the method of trial-and-error. . . . The art of political leadership demands the ability to uncover and effectively resolve contradictions—not to suppress them and let them accumulate, but to turn them into a source of

15. "Lavochka ili Kooperativ?" *Izvestiia,* October 3, 1987.

progress and self-development.''[16] Obviously the ultimate disaster would be that the steps led into a blind alley, for this would eventually produce the vote of no-confidence that Gorbachev had dared his opponents to introduce. But it was also necessary to calculate the political costs and benefits of the various partial steps and to try to time them so that benefits are seen before the more dangerous political actions are taken.

Logically the first steps of reform should be directed at loosening the supply system and bringing prices into line with the forces of supply and demand. Price irrationalities would have to be attacked before or simultaneously with a loosening of supply, for otherwise managers would be led to irrational production and purchasing decisions. Some of the most obvious problems arise in the realm of agriculture. Bread prices, for example, are lower than those of the grain used to produce it, while meat is sold for less than the peasants are paid for it. As a consequence, peasants who are free to follow their own economic self-interest should buy bread instead of grain to feed their pigs, and then they should sell the pigs to the state and buy their ham and bacon in the state stores. This is only one of the countless irrationalities that must be corrected.

Unfortunately from Gorbachev's point of view, the raising of key consumer prices is politically one of the most dangerous steps to take. In Poland the raising of meat prices produced riots, and, in practice, Gorbachev moved extremely cautiously to reform food prices. He opened the subject to fairly free discussion for the first time, but he did not raise prices in the state stores. Only in October 1987 did he finally, equivocally say that agricultural prices had to be raised, but he still did not say when. This necessarily slowed the pace of agricultural reform.

Nevertheless, the early stages of economic reform have to

16. *Pravda,* June 26, 1987.

introduce more flexibility into the supply and price system if they are to be effective. In the real world this normally means starting where supply relationships are the least complicated. In the economic conference of June 1987, Oleg Bogomolov pointed to the experience of the other socialist countries:

> This experience shows that the quickest and most direct effect for the people is produced by the application of economic methods of leadership first in agriculture, trade, the light and food industries, and in housing construction. . . . It is very characteristic that economic reforms . . . began in many countries precisely in agriculture. This was true in Hungary, China, and Czechoslovakia.[17]

The so-called Kosygin reforms of 1965 never did this, and they were doomed from the start.

The Gorbachev approach to agriculture was strange. He himself had endorsed the small-scale link as early as 1976,[18] and the framework for reform was introduced in the Brezhnev period. Small groups of peasants within the farm were encouraged to form "contract brigades" on a voluntary basis—brigades that would farm a particular section of collective farm land independently. If the brigades had really been voluntary, they would have been formed by families or small groups of friends. If they really functioned independently, the result would have been similar to the Chinese and Hungarian systems of family farming within a collective farm system. In fact, however, the contract brigades contained twenty-four persons on the average, and clearly were not voluntary;[19] the collective farm continued to receive an

---

17. *Pravda,* June 13, 1987.

18. V. P. Gagnon, Jr., "Gorbachev and the Collective Contract Brigade," *Soviet Studies,* vol. 39 (January 1987), pp. 1–23.

19. Tsentral'noe statisticheskoe upravlenie SSSR, *Narodnoe khoziaistvo SSSR v 1984 g.: statisticheskii ezhegodnik* (Moscow: Finansy i statistika, 1985), p. 327. These statistics were not published in comparable form in 1985.

extremely detailed plan, and hence could not permit any independence to its brigades, which do the farm's work.

Gorbachev had been Central Committee secretary for agriculture under Brezhnev, and he surely had the political authority to introduce any change in agriculture that he wanted after 1985—especially the end of formalism in a system that already existed. Moreover, he was able to select a very close associate from Stavropol as chief agricultural administrator, and at the Twenty-seventh Party Congress he endorsed extending the contract system, specifically referring to "brigades, links, and families, with the means of production, including land, being granted them for a contract period."[20]

In April 1986 collective farms were permitted to sell fruit and vegetables, including a significant part of their planned production, directly to the population at prices between those in the state stores and those in the collective farm markets. Stores that sold high-quality sausage at higher prices began to open. To the extent that this happened, it had the effect of raising the average price of goods without affecting the prices in state stores and of making the supply system more flexible. Yet in practice the collective farms remained under extreme regimentation, and neither the contract brigade nor the direct sales law had much more than symbolic effect, except to a very limited extent. Only in late 1987 did it appear that the leadership was ready to enact radical agricultural reform.

Reform in the services sector began earlier. In November 1986 the government passed a law legalizing individual labor after work or for housewives, students, and pensioners (men over sixty and women over fifty-five). They could not legally hire labor outside the family, but other laws were enacted that permitted larger groups to form cooperatives that would engage in the same kind of activities. A wide range of activities was permitted: the repair of apartments and cars, the provid-

20. *Pravda*, February 26, 1986.

ing of private medical care, bookbinding, private restaurants, tailoring, the production of small-scale industrial goods, small-scale construction, the use of private cars for taxis, and so forth. State enterprises were permitted and encouraged to make contracts with outside individuals who would work on a commission basis. In large part the illegal second economy was being legalized, and its expansion authorized.

Obviously the services reform could not become substantial unless significant access to state supplies was provided, but presumably this very fact would force the planners to include more supplies (including raw materials and industrial supplies) in stores that were available to all. Moreover, the legalization of the second economy made it possible for private individuals and groups to provide services more flexibly not only to the consumer but also to state enterprises. These would eventually include such extremely important services as production of computer software and business and financial consulting, which would make a serious difference in the performance of the state sector.

The movement toward legalization of the second economy served other important political purposes. First, of course, it provided the promise of an immediate payoff to the population in terms of improvements in the quality of life. It made it easier for the non-Russian populations to produce goods and services that corresponded to their national traditions, and hence gave them a sense of greater national autonomy from Moscow. Second, it provided the most ambitious and talented workers the opportunity to earn extra income immediately, which identified them with the reform. When the later, more difficult decisions that might produce worker opposition would be taken, the natural leadership of this opposition would have, it was hoped, already been co-opted. Third, insofar as problems in the industrial system created supply difficulties for the services sector, and this was inevitable, it would increase the political pressure for a more substantial industrial reform in several years.

Actually a series of steps was taken in the first two years of the Gorbachev regime to improve the performance of industry. Investment was increased, and a new quality control system was introduced. A substantial change of personnel may have energized the managerial cadres, and a number of small changes in the planning and incentive systems, as well as in the rights of enterprise directors, should have had some effect. Then the June 1987 plenum of the Central Committee focused more on industry. It approved the new state enterprise law and promised a restructuring of the central planning and administrative organs. Gorbachev talked about the replacement of administrative measures with economic ones, about "a fundamental change in the supply system—a movement from a centralized system to one based on wholesale trade in producers' goods," about "a radical reform of price formation," about "a radical financial-credit reform," and about a "cardinal" change of the functions of organs such as Gosplan.[21]

As far as could be judged, and Gorbachev was careful not to say this, the general secretary was looking at the Japanese economic model for inspiration. In the United States the automobile industry is one of the few in which the industrial producer also has retail outlets that specialize in its products and services them as well. This pattern is far more general in Japan, and Gorbachev endorsed it. There should be, he said, "several thousand important branch, interbranch, and territorial-branch firms, capable of carrying out the whole cycle: scientific research, investment, production, sales and service." These big firms should be supplemented by tens of thousands of small enterprises, either cooperative or subordinated to local government, that would serve the big firms and the local market.[22] The director of the Institute of Economics, Leonid Abalkin, in a post-plenum interview with

21. *Pravda,* June 26, 1987.
22. Ibid.

Der Spiegel, pointed to Japanese strategic planning, which in his view would be the model for Gosplan in the Soviet Union.[23]

In addition, Gorbachev talked about a change in the economic system that would, indeed, gradually introduce flexibility into the supply system. Instead of having Gosplan and the ministries give the enterprises a production plan with items included in it, the new system would be based largely on orders from purchasing bodies. Some of these orders would come from the state and would be obligatory, some from other state enterprises, and some from cooperatives or individuals.

Whether or not this was true, the extent of reform would depend on the proportion of industry's production that would be determined by state orders. If it was 90 percent or more, the old system would be preserved, but with "orders" being a different name for "chits" or "directives." If the only government orders were for the defense industry, foreign aid, and the like, then the system might not be that different in this respect from the West. Gorbachev declared that in 1988 enterprises which produced two-thirds of all industrial production would be working on the new principles of management and that the transition to the new system would be completed by 1989. Abel Aganbegian, the chief scholarly strategist of the economic reform, told a Swedish newspaper that the percentage of state orders in an enterprise's plan would soon fall to 50–60 percent and then to 30 percent by 1990.[24] Abalkin also used the 30 percent figure, but for a vague "first phase" of reform, and added that there would be no state orders in light industry.[25]

It is probably wise to be cautious about the speed of the

23. *Der Speigel,* July 6, 1987, in *FBIS-SU,* July 10, 1987, pp. S1, S3.

24. *Dagens Nyheter* (Stockholm), June 28, 1987, in *FBIS-SU,* July 13, 1987, p. R16.

25. *Der Speigel,* July 6, 1987, in *FBIS-SU,* July 10, 1987, p. S3.

industrial reform, especially outside of light industry. Light industry has officially been working on a system of wholesale trade, but, as even the supposedly conservative Yegor Ligachev complained in 1986, this still has little real meaning. Further, no one was promising a completion of radical financial and price reform by 1989. These points should be remembered over the next year or so when the reform does not go as fast as the reformers want, and westerners again begin talking about some powerful opposition to Gorbachev.

Despite all the talk about industry at the plenum, the extent of state ownership should not be forgotten: state farms, state stores, and even movie theaters. At the June plenum Gorbachev spoke at length about family farming within the collective farm system and strongly suggested that the time had passed when the laws on individual labor and cooperatives should be questioned. It is likely that the real meaning of the June plenum was an acceleration of the services reform and the beginning of a radical transformation of the collective farm system. At a minimum, however, Gorbachev was showing that he had a well-conceived economic strategy that could lead to major industrial reform by the early 1990s.

Even if Gorbachev succeeds in introducing far more domestic competitiveness into the Soviet economic system, the massive protection from foreign competition enjoyed by Soviet manufacturers would remain as a major cause of the technological problems that Gorbachev decried. If the attack on protectionism were postponed until the 1990s, the pace of reform would be very slow. In fact, in 1987 the new regime began an attack on protectionism as well. It announced an export strategy in manufactured goods to replace the Brezhnev policy of importing machinery and exporting commodities. For the first time since the 1920s, the government passed a law on joint ventures that permits foreign ownership inside the Soviet Union. These changes, and their foreign policy implications, deserve a chapter to themselves.

4

Foreign Economic Policy

ONE of the strangest aspects of American analysis of the Soviet Union has been its neglect of Soviet foreign economic policy. It has simply been taken for granted that the Soviet Union is limited to the choice between importing and not importing foreign technology; the debates have then centered on whether the United States should accommodate any such desire and at what price. But that is all.

Yet when analysts consider the foreign economic policies of other countries, including the United States, they are absorbed with the question of protectionism. The American intellectual tradition has strongly emphasized free trade as a key to economic performance, and one would expect a tendency to explain Soviet economic difficulties by its totally protectionist policies. In practice, no one—not even economists specializing in the Soviet Union—has focused on this factor, even though in the 1970s Soviet manufacturers were far more protected than the Japanese. Instead, scholars wrote about "the decision to terminate regional autarchy," about movement "a long way toward reversing the historic East-West economic separation."[1]

There are many explanations for this phenomenon. First, of course, Soviet trade with the West did increase substan-

1. Valerie Bunce, "The Empire Strikes Back: The Transformation of the Eastern Bloc from a Soviet Asset to a Soviet Liability," *International Organization,* vol. 39 (Winter 1985), p. 2; and David Ost, "Socialist World Market as Strategy for Ascent?" in Edward Friedman, ed., *Ascent and Decline in the World-System* (Sage Publications, 1982), p. 246.

tially in the 1970s, and this was a significant break with the past. The scale of trade with the developed capitalist world increased from 1.9 billion rubles in 1960 to 4.7 billion in 1970 to 31.6 billion in 1980.[2] It was easy to forget, however, that much of this increase was simply the result of a tenfold rise in the price of the two main Soviet exports, gold and petroleum (or natural gas), between 1970 and 1980.

Second, Soviet protectionism was embodied in the very essence of its economic system, and was not the result of highly visible tariffs and embargoes. Moreover, western analysis of Soviet economic problems comes largely from debates in the Soviet media, and even the most radical Soviet reform economists never discussed protectionism as a problem in the Soviet system. Until 1987 they almost never directly suggested that the introduction of foreign competition was important—and even now only rarely.

One reason was that most Soviet economists were slow to understand the problem. They were trained in the Leninist analysis of capitalism ("imperialism") that treated foreign economic relations between the western capitalist world and less developed countries as inherently exploitative. They saw a strong element of dependence—even semicolonial dependence—in these relations, which scarcely suggested that the Soviet Union should go the same route. The experience of Pacific and third world countries in the 1970s and the 1980s led to a change in perception among Soviet specialists on the outside world, but this understanding apparently did not diffuse quickly among Soviet economists studying the domestic scene.

Probably even more important, reformers who did understand the need to attack protectionism have been reluctant to say so in print, lest it increase opposition to reform. As has

2. Ministerstvo vneshnei torgovli SSSR, *Vneshniaia torgovlia Soiuza SSR za 1959–1963 gody: statisticheskii sbornik* (Moscow: Vneshtorgizdat, 1965), p. 11; *Vneshniaia torgovlia za 1971*, p. 10; and *Vneshniaia torgovlia v 1981*, p. 8.

been seen, the central purpose of the Soviet political-eco-
nomic system was to protect an anxious population against
western ideas and unsettling market forces, especially foreign
ones.

As a consequence, a major change in Soviet foreign
economic policy is an extraordinarily sensitive political issue,
and the care with which Gorbachev has handled it should
come as no surprise. A real opening of the Soviet Union to
the world economy involves competition with foreign firms,
whose workers have long been said to be exploited by
bloodsucking capitalists. If foreign investment inside the
Soviet Union is contemplated, Soviet workers may be directly subject to the supervision of such capitalists. If plan
fulfillment is made dependent on the exportation of manufactured goods, then Soviet factories must produce for the
changing tastes of foreign populations, information about
whom has been strictly controlled and censored for sixty
years.

Not surprisingly, Gorbachev treated the subject gingerly.
In May 1985 he implicitly praised East German foreign
economic policy (that is, East Germany's use of its access to
the West German market to force its manufacturers to produce goods closer to world levels of quality), but this statement was cut from the published version of the speech. When
the Soviet Union legalized foreign investment in the Soviet
Union through joint ventures in January 1987, the law was
enacted without any prior public discussion.[3] It was published
on the day that the Central Committee plenum on democra-

3. Even many top scholars were not brought into the detailed,
behind-the-scenes discussions on the law and the policy. In late
November 1986 I was shown a printed copy of the joint venture law
at a distance and was told that joint ventures should be based on
existing enterprises rather than on new construction, at least at first.
A top Soviet economic specialist on Japan insisted in another interview
that joint ventures based on existing enterprises were not even being
considered.

tization opened, and hence went virtually unnoticed in the
avalanche of publicity on the plenum.

But precisely because protectionism in the Soviet Union
has had all the consequences predicted by free trade text-
books, a transformation of foreign economic policy is indispensable for a successful economic reform. The problem for
western analysts is now and will continue to be a difficult
one: how to understand the precise nature of the change in
policy when the Soviet leadership has such a strong interest
in camouflaging its more frightening aspects from the Soviet
population.

Changes in Policy

During the 1960s and 1970s the issue of the state monopoly
of trade was raised "constantly" (to use the word of a Soviet
trade official), and a top institute director argued privately
that it did not mean the monopoly of the Ministry of Foreign
Trade. Nevertheless, the Soviet leadership consistently rejected this pressure. When the U.S. Commerce Department
proposed in 1973 that the Soviet Union join the General
Agreement on Trade and Tariffs (GATT) and attend the
Tokyo round, the Soviet Union declined to take even this
modest step.

Yet behind the scenes, major changes in perception were
occurring. Some economists began talking about the advan-
tages of the "international division of labor" in ways that
implicitly went well beyond the earlier endorsements of
foreign trade.[4] Beliefs about the semicolonial and dependent
position of third world countries that accepted foreign investment and the marketplace were subjected to increasing
attack. By the early 1980s the overwhelming majority of
serious Soviet economists working on the third world even

4. See Elizabeth Kridl Valkenier, *The Soviet Union and the Third
World: An Economic Bind* (Praeger, 1983), pp. 37–69 and 109–43.

argued that integration of such countries into the world economy led to stronger growth than autarky and "socialist orientation."[5]

The rules of censorship prevented Soviet third world specialists from stating flatly that the experience of these developing countries was relevant for Soviet domestic policy, but the implication was often clear. Consider the following statement by Ivan Ivanov, then deputy director of the Institute of World Economics and International Relations (IMEMO), which reversed the old argument on dependence:

> The young states . . . all the more often receive access to the technical-financial potential of the transnational corporation while preserving national sovereignty over natural resources and their economies. . . . So far as the transnational corporation is concerned, the profits they receive . . . are dependent in much greater degree on the work of their subsidiaries.[6]

Ivanov poured scorn on the "simplified" notion of "non-equivalent trade," which "has already been repeatedly disproved," and he defined world market prices as the "socially necessary ones." He explicitly advocated that Soviet enterprises farm out production of components to third world companies—a policy that seemed also to imply the desirability of joint production with firms in the industrial world.[7]

Ivanov was widely know as a reformer, but a scholar with a conservative reputation, Anatolii Dinkevich, came even closer to a direct indictment of the entire Soviet foreign economic policy and system:

> A course toward a closed economy or, in other words, toward economic autarky is, as history shows, a course without a

5. This is discussed in Jerry F. Hough, *The Struggle for the Third World: Soviet Debates and American Options* (Brookings, 1986), pp. 70–104.

6. "Gosudarstvo i inostrannyi kapital: modifikatsiia otnosheniia," *Aziia i Afrika segodnia,* no. 2 (1984), p. 31.

7. "Transnatsional'nye korporatsii i razvivaiushchiisia mir," *Latinskaia Amerika,* no. 8 (1983), pp. 49–50.

future. It is a path leading to a dead end. . . . Characteristically, the higher the level of participation in the system of the international division of labor, the higher the tempos of economic growth. . . . Extreme protectionism, carried out over an unjustifiably long time, is fraught with negative consequences (the preservation and extension of backward, noncompetitive, inefficient production, with high costs, low productivity of labor, and low quality production).[8]

From a policy point of view, the important thing was not that such statements passed censorship, but that they won such wide support among specialists. They were seldom challenged directly, and then only on the ground that growth was achieved at the expense of the more important value of "social justice." The scholars who made these strong statements about the prerequisites of economic growth were fairly high members of the policy-oriented world, and they were looking to their future careers. It is hard to believe that the community would have swung so far to one side in criticizing current Soviet policy if it had not had a sense that its views were shared by the successor generation of high officialdom.[9]

In fact, this new perspective was beginning to have some minor impact on policy even in the late Brezhnev period. Foreign trade "reforms" in 1978 and 1979 formalized industrial participation in the specialized foreign trade organs of the Ministry of Foreign Trade.[10] In 1982 the Soviet Union reversed its position on membership in GATT. Such steps,

---

8. A. I. Dinkevich, "O strategii ekonomicheskogo razvitiia osvobodivshikhsia stran," in A. I. Dinkevich, *Razvivaiushchiesia strany: nakoplenie i ekonomicheskii rost* (Moscow: Nauka, 1977), pp. 8, 12.

9. Indeed, the battle between Andropov and Chernenko was fought on the issue of growth versus social justice, and the retreat of the conservative third world specialists to the social justice position reflected this political reality.

10. Ed A. Hewett, "Foreign Economic Relations," in Abram Bergson and Herbert S. Levine, eds., *The Soviet Economy: Toward the Year 2000* (Allen and Unwin, 1983), pp. 297–98.

however, had little practical significance. The chairman of the dominant foreign economic commission of the Council of Ministers was Ivan Arkhipov, a Brezhnev crony from the 1930s who celebrated his seventy-fifth birthday in 1982. The minister of foreign trade, Nikolai Patolichev, only one year younger, had been elected a voting member of the Central Committee in 1941 and appointed minister of foreign trade in 1958. Foreign economic policy was not going to change meaningfully as long as they retained their posts. That they kept their posts indicated that Brezhnev did not want a policy change.

With the election of Mikhail Gorbachev, however, it became increasingly clear that the Soviet specialists on the third world had made a winning political bet. As early as June 1985 Gorbachev had damned the noncompetitive character of Soviet manufactured goods in the world market and the low level of exports, stating flatly, "It is impossible to tolerate this any longer."[11] Nevertheless, during the new general secretary's first year in office, he was cautious in his foreign economic policy statements, let alone in his actions. Although Patolichev was retired as foreign trade minister in 1985, he was replaced by a man who was not inspiring on the surface— a former Leningrad party official who had been serving as deputy minister of foreign affairs for Eastern Europe. Even at the Twenty-seventh Party Congress, Gorbachev said relatively little about foreign economic questions, but the chairman of the Council of Ministers, Nikolai Ryzhkov, was more insistent about shifting to the exportation of manufactured goods instead of commodities.

It was after the Twenty-seventh Congress that the pace of change picked up. The Politburo's commission on economic reform, headed by the chairman of Gosplan, Nikolai Talyzin, was composed of high officials, most of whom were probably lukewarm at best about reform. The commission, however, had a scientific section (*nauchnaia sektsiia*) that consisted

11. *Pravda,* June 12, 1985.

of some twenty-five leading scholars—usually institute directors or their designated representatives. This section created working groups on all aspects of the reform, and they drew in scholars from a range of interested departments and institutions. It is said that the Academy of Sciences' Institute of State and Law, for example, has been doing little else except assist in the drafting of various pieces of reform legislation, and the Institute on the Economics of the World Socialist System had a large role in drafting foreign economic legislation.

During 1986 the first major steps were taken to transform the institutional framework of foreign economic policy. The foreign economic commission of the Council of Ministers, supervised by a deputy chairman of the Council of Ministers, had long coordinated foreign economic policy. Now it became a formal institution of the Council of Ministers. The precise meaning of this change is not clear, but it involved an increase in both authority and staff. The former Commission of the Presidium of the Council of Ministers for Comecon Questions was apparently merged into the foreign economic commission, and the staff of the business office (*upravlenie delami*), which normally drafted legislation,[12] apparently lost this function. By late 1986 the new staff stood at some 100 persons, and a new research institute was created and attached to the commission (the All-Union Scientific-Research Institute of Foreign Economic Ties—VNIIVS) to provide it with additional expertise.

The truly important development in the foreign economic

12. M. S. Smirtiukov, *Sovetskii gosudarstvennyi apparat upravleniia,* 2d ed. (Moscow: Politizdat, 1984), p. 208, reported that "the Business Office carries out the preparations of questions for consideration in the Council of Ministers." For the reference to the Commission (*Komissiia Prezidiuma Soveta Ministrov SSSR po voprosam Soveta Ekonomicheskoi Vzaimopomoshchi*), see *Sobranie postanovlenii pravitel'stva Soiuza Sovetskikh Sotsialisticheskikh Respublik,* no. 31 (Moscow: Izdanie upravleniia delami Soveta Ministrov SSSR, 1985), p. 613, statute 149.

commission was a personnel change. Brezhnev's old conservative crony Arkhipov was replaced as chairman by
Vladimir Kamentsev, the former minister of the fishing
industry. Kamentsev not only had some experience with joint
ventures and foreign economic negotiations but also had been
working directly under Mikhail Gorbachev when he was
Central Committee secretary for agriculture and the food
industry in the Brezhnev period.

The new deputy chairman of the commission was even
more interesting. He was Ivan Ivanov, the highly critical and
innovative scholar of the Brezhnev years who had spoken
out on the benefits to third world countries of foreign investment.[13] In essence, with Kamentsev an administrator and his
first deputy the chief Soviet representative to Comecon,
Ivanov became the country's de facto top foreign economic
strategist. When he had been deputy director of IMEMO, the
director of the institute under whom he served from September 1983 to July 1985 was Aleksandr Yakovlev. Yakovlev
became Gorbachev's chief strategist for domestic and foreign
policy in 1985 and rose rapidly in the formal political hierarchy. (He was head of the propaganda—really media—
department of the Central Committee in July 1985, Central
Committee secretary in March 1986, candidate member of
the Politburo in February 1987, and full Politburo member in
June 1987.) As Politburo member and Central Committee
secretary for ideology and foreign relations, Yakovlev now
occupies the crucial slot in the system that had been held for
years by Mikhail Suslov and then in 1982 by Yurii Andropov.
Ivanov in a real sense has to be Yakovlev's man in developing
and carrying out foreign economic strategy, and ultimately
he must have enormous potential power in bureaucratic
conflicts.

13. The first deputy chairman, A. K. Antonov, was formally the
most powerful deputy, but he was the seventy-five-year-old Soviet
representative to Comecon and concentrated on trade with Eastern
Europe.

In 1986 the Ministry of Foreign Affairs also acted to increase its role in foreign economic policy. It had had a department (*otdel*) for international economic organizations, but the Soviet Union had usually not joined such international decisionmaking organizations as the International Monetary Fund (IMF) and World Bank; rather, it has joined United Nations–related ones. Hence the department's role had primarily been one of articulating official Soviet positions, which often were propagandistic, instead of policymaking. In November 1986 the ministry upgraded the department to a larger administration or bureau (*upravlenie*), and renamed it the Foreign Economic Administration to indicate that its role went beyond international organizations. The head of the administration was placed on the collegium of the ministry, and he was subordinated to the deputy minister for Latin America, not the deputy minister for international organizations.

But again the crucial fact was a personnel change. The man appointed head of the new administration was Ernest Obminsky, a scholar who had been a leader in the movement to recognize the importance of the international division of labor.[14] Obminsky too had worked previously in IMEMO, under Ivanov and Yakovlev. Hence he too was part of the inner advisory directorate on foreign economic questions, and the role of the institution that hired him rose correspondingly.

Another institution whose role in foreign economic relations increased was the State Committee on Foreign Economic Ties. Formerly it had been largely limited to providing economic aid and military assistance to third world and socialist countries, especially when construction or assemblying operations were required. In 1986 the committee was given the right to serve as the general contractor for foreign

14. See Valkenier, *The Soviet Union and the Third World*, pp. 83–84; and Hough, *The Struggle for the Third World*, p. 99, note 96.

construction inside the Soviet Union as well as outside. In particular, the committee would be the agency responsible for the construction of joint ventures in the Soviet Union that required significant new structures. A former Central Committee secretary and deputy chairman of the Council of Ministers, the fifty-eight-year-old Konstantin Katushev, was appointed chairman of the committee, replacing a seventy-six-year-old with decades of work in the institution. There were indications that the committee would be entrepreneurial in this role, both in persuading foreigners that its construction was of much higher quality than that of the old domestic ministries and in pushing Soviet authorities to a large-scale program of new joint-venture construction.

Other institutions became more powerful in foreign economic policy simply because they upgraded their personnel. For example, the head of the foreign currency–economic research administration of the State Bank—the international division—in 1987 was a forty-year-old, Yurii V. Ponomarev, who had worked in Soviet banks abroad and could speak an international business English that seemed as sophisticated as that of a western counterpart. Beginning in 1988 the State Bank was to become independent of and a competitor to the Foreign Trade Bank.

By far the most important change was an attack in 1986 on the monopoly position of the Ministry of Foreign Trade. The ministry retained responsibility for importing and exporting such undifferentiated products as petroleum and grain, but trade in manufactured goods was largely transferred to twenty-one industrial ministries and seventy (later seventy-five) very large industrial enterprises.[15] By July 1987 the Ministry of the Electrotechnical Industry, for example, had a special foreign trade corporation (*ob"edinenie*), Sovelektro, with 400 employees.[16]

15. *Pravda,* September 24, 1986; the figure of seventy-five is given in *Literaturnaia gazeta,* July 8, 1987. (Hereafter *Lit. gaz.*)

16. V. Shmyganovsky, "'Sovelektro': pervye shagi," *Izvestiia,* July 25, 1987.

In the past enterprise directors had had almost no interest in producing for the export market. To change this situation, the government decided to assign a certain percentage of foreign currency earnings to the ministry or enterprise responsible for them. The percentage varies with the complexity of the product. Supposedly the economic managers are free to use these earnings for anything for the factory—machinery or toilet paper, to quote one official. Firms—even small ones—are being encouraged to enter into joint enterprises with foreign firms, again with the right of retaining some of the currency for their own use. Most important of all, factory managers who enter the foreign market independently will now be the ones who travel abroad to negotiate contracts, to see foreign plants, to seek foreign customers. Only those who take foreign travel for granted can fail to imagine the enormity of this incentive.

In June 1986 the Soviet Union sent a formal letter to GATT seeking membership. Hints were dropped about an eventual interest in membership in the IMF and the World Bank, and a high official was sent to Washington to conduct soundings. Third world policy began to deemphasize radicals and to focus more on economic and government relations with the wealthier industrializing countries in the area. In June 1986 the Soviet Union began a partial cooperation with the Organization of Petroleum Exporting Countries, or OPEC (apparently now suspended), and its later offer to provide protection to Kuwaiti ships was part of this policy. The subordination of the foreign economic administration of the Ministry of Foreign Affairs to the deputy minister for Latin America hinted at the importance to be given to countries such as Argentina, Brazil, and Mexico in relations with that continent. Eduard Shevardnadze's visit to the first two in September 1987 dramatized the point.

In his speech on the seventieth anniversary of the Bolshevik revolution in November 1987, Gorbachev specifically damned Trotsky for his "pseudo-revolutionary" policy of exporting revolution and labeled it defeatist. Stalin had also called Trotsky defeatist by asserting (falsely) that the latter's espousal of world revolution meant that Russia could do nothing on its own.[17] In 1987, however, Gorbachev was saying that a foreign policy that concentrated on revolution in such countries as Angola, Ethiopia, and Nicaragua, and on communist parties elsewhere, was conceding the big, nonrevolutionary countries such as Argentina, Brazil, Egypt, India, Indonesia, and Mexico to the United States—and giving up on the prerequisites for an attack on protectionism that Soviet economic development required.

Joint Ventures

Politically the most explosive new foreign economic measure was the legalization—and encouragement—of joint production with capitalist firms and of foreign investment inside the Soviet Union. Lenin had permitted a tiny amount of foreign investment in the 1920s, especially in raw materials industries, but this experiment was short-lived. Modern Russians have no personal experience with capitalism, only the stereotypes about exploitative capitalism, reinforced in the Soviet press for decades. The idea that Soviet workers should actually be employed in capitalist-managed plants is inevitably quite frightening.

The decision to permit joint ventures in the Soviet Union had been moving forward behind the scene long before the idea was even timidly broached in public. By the end of 1985 the Hamburg Institute for Eastern Market Research had been told that Gorbachev favored joint ventures and that a Council of Ministers decision was being prepared.[18] Joint ventures with socialist countries were formally endorsed in August 1986. The State Committee on Foreign Economic Ties had received the right to supervise domestic foreign construction,

17. *Pravda,* November 3, 1987.
18. Hamburg DPA, January 8, 1986, in Foreign Broadcast Information Service, *Daily Report: Soviet Union,* January 10, 1986, p. S1.

and soon a special department for joint ventures was established within the Ministry of Foreign Trade. By the end of November the Supreme Soviet law on joint ventures was already in typed form. The Politburo formally approved it on December 25, 1986, and the Presidium of the Supreme Soviet on January 13, 1987. The law was published on January 27.[19]

Publication of the joint venture law coincided with the opening of the Central Committee plenum on democratization, but "coincided" did not mean "coincidental." Not only did publication come two weeks after the adoption of the law, but I had been told in November that the law would be published in mid-December. The Central Committee plenum had originally been scheduled for that time, but had been postponed—presumably because of riots in Kazakhstan and Beijing. There were several reasons for the timing of the joint venture law. First, as already noted, the democratization plenum, with its promise of the election of factory managers, preempted public attention from an explosive issue for workers. Second, an implicit deal was being offered the middle class, the bureaucrats: a freer society, with more travel abroad, at the price of a more difficult life at work, including pressure from foreign competition.

Many activities may be subsumed under the term *joint ventures*. The chairman of the State Foreign Economic Commission estimates that nearly 50 percent of Common Market production involves international joint production.[20] Although this joint production seldom extends to the socialist world, Volkswagen has some of its motors produced in East Germany. The Soviet Union has engaged in such activity with India and wants to extend the practice. In addition, jointly owned Soviet enterprises can be created with Eastern

19. *Pravda,* December 26, 1986, and January 27, 1987. For a description of the first major joint venture with a machine-tool plant, see *Pravda,* July 14, 1987.

20. *Lit. gaz.,* July 8, 1987.

European partners as well as capitalist ones, and over thirty are expected by the end of 1987.[21]

The joint ventures of greatest interest to the West, however, are those involving western ownership. Unfortunately, even though the joint venture law was published in January 1987, its exact meaning remains uncertain, as does the vigor with which it will be pushed. A Brookings-led group of businessmen that visited the Soviet Union in June 1987 met officials of ten Soviet institutions with direct or indirect involvement in the program and repeatedly heard such answers as "we don't know yet," "that's still to be decided," "there are gray areas and even blank spots in the law," and so forth. Sometimes an answer given in one interview would contradict an answer given in another.

Nevertheless, some aspects of the policy, at least of current policy, are clear. Foreigners will not be allowed to own outright factories or other enterprises in the Soviet Union. While the law specifies that the "ownership" will always be 51 percent–49 percent, it would be wrong to assume that the Soviet Union will make a 51 percent cash investment and the foreign partner 49 percent. Normally the foreigner's contribution is to come in the form of the imported equipment for the venture, and the Soviet contribution is to be the building, the roads, and so forth. Each is responsible for obtaining the credit necessary for its own contribution. The mandatory Soviet majority share means that the chairman of the board and the managing director must be Soviets, but the contract can specify the need for unanimous agreement by both partners on certain questions and this apparently is occurring often.

From the point of view of the foreigner, the most important aspect of the joint venture is that it must be self-sufficient in its foreign currency accounts. That is, the foreign currency used for the salaries of foreigners, for imported supplies, for

21. Ibid.

other expenditures incurred abroad, and for the repatriated profits of the foreign partner must be covered by currency earned in foreign sales (or hard-currency sales to foreigners in the Soviet Union). There have been hints that this rule might be relaxed somewhat when the joint venture is producing goods for the Soviet domestic market that otherwise would have to be imported for hard currency, but the authorities thus far have been reluctant to confirm the possibility of such an exception.[22]

Joint ventures can be formed in a wide range of economic activities, and services for foreign tourists (for example, hotels) are a natural area for cooperation. Even joint ventures providing services primarily or exclusively for the Soviet domestic market are possible theoretically, but only if the foreign partner is willing to take its profit in the form of some Soviet product that it then sells abroad.[23] The Soviet Union, furthermore, has a special interest in high-technology areas that would help achieve the goals of reducing agricultural imports or bringing the Soviet Union closer to world levels of technology. In November 1986 a high Soviet official suggested that the Soviet Union was going to give priority to a few crucial spheres—agro-chemistry, machinebuilding, and

22. If the Soviet Union is paying $1 million in hard currency to import fertilizer, for example, it makes theoretical sense to encourage the construction of a joint venture to end this import and then to permit the repatriation of $1 million profit (or some percentage of it) beyond foreign earnings, treating the reduced export expenditures as part of currency self-sufficiency. In practice, of course, every firm will be arguing that its particular product is import substitution that saves foreign currency and, therefore, is deserving of special treatment.

23. Pepsi-Cola has been providing syrup for the domestic production of its product in the Soviet Union. In return, it sells Stolichnaia vodka in the United States. A foreign currency balance is maintained between the two products. This particular countertrade operation is not a joint venture, as presently discussed, but the analogy could be applied in joint ventures.

pulp and paper—but an October 1987 decree put more emphasis on the services.[24]

Joint ventures, it should be emphasized, need not be limited to government plants and ministries. The new private cooperatives that are now possible under Gorbachev's reforms may, theoretically at least, also take foreign partners in some aspects of their activities, and one of the first joint ventures reportedly involved a Finnish firm and an Estonian clothing cooperative. Soviet analysts have a clear sense that the introduction of inventions and scientific discoveries into production has been a weak point in the Soviet system, and they profoundly hope that western and third world firms will enter into joint ventures with Soviet scientific institutes to bring Soviet technological innovations to life. Some Soviet scholars have privately suggested the possibility of joint ventures with Soviet scientists who form private cooperatives.[25]

When Americans hear of 51 percent–49 percent joint ventures, they tend to think of new factory construction. In fact, Soviet policy is currently based on a different assumption. Although the Soviet phrase *sovmestnoe predpriiatie* would normally be translated "joint enterprise" or "joint plant," the official Soviet translation is "joint venture," and a real point is being made. A "joint enterprise" conveys the image of a new factory, but in fact, preference is to be given at first to foreign investment within existing Soviet plants. An existing shop may be emptied of old machinery and supplied with the equipment from the foreign partner. The plant or enterprise in such cases will not be a joint one, only the venture in the shop.

There are several reasons for this approach. First, a joint venture within an existing plant can be relatively small at

24. *Ekonomicheskaia gazeta,* no. 41 (October 1987), pp. 18–19. (Hereafter *Ekon. gaz.*)

25. Thomas H. Naylor, "Gorbachev Says 'Radical Reform'—and Means It," *New York Times,* June 27, 1987.

first. It can become operational quickly and produce results more rapidly at minimum cost to the Soviet Union. Second, if existing buildings are used, they become part of the Soviet 51 percent contribution, reducing the Soviet Union's need for new construction. Third, the foreigner can provide foreign marketing expertise not only for the products of the joint venture itself but also for the whole plant to which the venture is attached. Fourth, engineers, junior managers, and workers can easily be shifted back and forth between the mother plant and the joint venture, thereby diffusing knowledge of western managerial techniques. Fifth, labor discontent in an isolated joint enterprise may build up and explode, but unhappy workers in a joint venture attached to an existing plant can easily be shifted to a different, Soviet-owned shop and replaced by others without any formal hiring and firing process.

Although the outlines of the joint venture program are fairly clear, a great number of details remain vague. For example, Soviet domestic prices are often artificial, and the ruble is not convertible. How will the Soviet 51 percent contribution to the joint venture and the cost of Soviet labor and supplies be priced? How are the quality of Soviet supplies and their timely delivery to be guaranteed? Will the foreign partner have the ability to select and retain the Soviet engineers and workers it wants? How will legal restrictions against transferring information to foreign governments be reconciled with foreign requirements of reports for income tax and export control purposes? Will the foreign firm be able to obtain visas for U.S. citizens who emigrated from the Soviet Union in recent years and whom the firm may want to hire for their knowledge of the Soviet bureaucratic maze? If the venture is liquidated, how is the value of the foreigner's portion to be evaluated? The list is virtually endless.

Some of these problems can be solved easily with changes in the law. (This surely will be done to permit the foreign partner to submit the necessary income tax information, for example.) Some can be resolved in the contracts signed in establishing the individual joint venture. Others, however, require major changes in Soviet political and legal traditions. For example, Soviet contract law must be changed to provide the flexibility needed for market-oriented activities; it now gives little opportunity for contracts by socialist enterprises outside the plan. A new institute for the study of international law is apparently to be established, and in large part it will work on international business law.

In addition, the Soviet Union must abandon the kind of obsession with secrecy that has often prevented western suppliers from seeing Soviet plants and that prohibits foreigners from taking photographs of economic enterprises (even grain elevators) and bridges (even inside Moscow). The Soviet Union must become more relaxed about issuing visas so that joint enterprise Soviet personnel may visit the plant and home office of the foreign partner or even so that Soviet citizens can seek foreign partners. In the spring of 1987 visas began to be issued to the "third wave" emigrants of the 1970s, but the process must become more automatic. If Soviet leaders find these types of changes politically or psychologically impossible, then neither the joint venture program nor the economic reform as a whole will succeed.

Prospects for Foreign Economic Reform

Ultimately a serious attack on Soviet protectionism will require radical change in the Soviet incentive and planning system. Complaints have already appeared that the new rules on the foreign trade powers of the ministries "in no way correspond to the economic reforms" and that the powers of the firms must be increased.[26] Moreover, as long as the

26. Shmyganovsky, " 'Sovelektro.' " A Central Committee de-

process of supplies procurement creates excessive demand by its very nature, Soviet plants will have only limited incentive to export. Only as the basic power relations between the ministry and enterprises are resolved will their respective rights and interests in foreign trade also be clarified.

After analyzing the tentative nature of the early industrial reform and reading (and hearing) complaints about the new laws, most western observers have been skeptical about the meaningfulness and seriousness of Gorbachev's reform in the foreign economic sphere and doubtful about such phrases as "attack on protectionism," which is used in this book.

Western skepticism about Soviet foreign economic reform has been heightened by a strong tendency to focus most attention on the new joint venture law. Its ambiguities and problems, which are many and visible, have been emphasized, as has been the relative smallness of the program in 1987. Although the exact number of joint ventures is difficult to ascertain, since many Soviets themselves apply the term to joint undertakings not involving 51 percent–49 percent ownership and management, it appears that only eight had formally been approved by the late summer of 1987. The first joint venture agreement with a U.S. firm was signed in early November 1987, and it was authoritatively stated that twenty to twenty-five with western firms and a comparable number with socialist firms would be signed by the end of the year. There would then be a pause for evaluation.

While cautionary warnings are in order, in my judgment the seriousness of Gorbachev's foreign economic reforms today are being as seriously underestimated as were his domestic reform intentions in 1985—indeed perhaps even more so. In the first place, the centrality of joint ventures should not be exaggerated. In a symbolic sense the joint

cree of October 1987 made a similar point and tried to simplify the process. *Ekon. gaz.*, no. 41 (October 1987).

venture is extraordinarily important, for nothing better dramatizes—both at home and abroad—the change in attitude toward the outside world than the decision to permit foreign investment on Soviet soil. Nevertheless, the joint venture is only one aspect of the foreign economic program, and in quantitative terms such measures as an export strategy, the encouragement of licensing arrangements, joint production without joint ownership, and the like will be more important.

Exports will be the center of the program. In the past, Soviet exports of manufactured goods—outside of weapons—have been limited. Little attention has been given them. When the Soviet Union began exporting Lada automobiles to Canada in 1981, it sold over 15,000 the first year, but the number fell to about 2,000 in 1986. No model changes had been introduced, and a reliable service network with a reliable supply of spare parts had not been established.[27] With the new program, this situation will change, and the significance of this fact should not be underestimated. Even a centrally enforced export strategy will have an impact, and export earnings are now included in the plan.[28] East German industry has benefited from its exposure to foreign competition, despite a planning system similar to the Soviet Union's, and the Soviet Union will be no different.

Nor should western analysts neglect the importance of the joint production program. Multinational corporations often obtain parts and semiprocessed raw materials throughout the world—often in countries with less-skilled work forces than that of the Soviet Union. If the Soviet Union sets the prices of labor and materials competitively, it can make such activity profitable for foreign firms. Joint production provides many of the benefits of joint ventures to the Soviet Union and

27. I. Dorofeev, "Byt' li 'Lade' v Kanade?" *Lit. gaz.,* September 9, 1987.
28. V. Kamentsev, "Problemy vneshneekonomicheskoi deiatel'-nosti," *Kommunist,* no. 15 (October 1987), pp. 25–34.

automatically solves many of the problems of the repatriation of profits. The exported parts are the "profits."

The new system of orders in Soviet industry, if effective, will change the situation dramatically. The gradual process of opening Soviet industry to domestic competition will be facilitated by the possibility of foreign entrants and by the ability of Soviet firms to use foreign currency to buy imports to replace a low-quality Soviet supplier—or even to threaten to do so. Just as Soviet industrial reform over the next ten years must be judged on its success in making incremental but steady progress, so must the attack on protectionism be similarly judged.

In the second place, western analysts—and the Soviet officials and intellectuals with whom they talk—are exaggerating the importance of the institutional interests of the "bureaucracy" and underestimating the importance of the individual interests of the "bureaucrats." They are exaggerating the economic interests of the "bureaucrats" in a stable job situation, and they are forgetting everything that they know about analogous educated, middle-class people abroad. Such people, including the author and no doubt readers of this book, want interesting, challenging jobs rather than dull, stable ones. Our interests are not limited to our jobs; we also want informative newspapers, the right to travel, the right to be autonomous of a specific bureaucratic hierarchy, the right to become rich, and so forth. Even if we do not exercise these rights, we want the opportunity for ourselves and our children to do so.

In no area do these personal interests of the bureaucrats conflict with the institutional interests of the bureaucracies more than in the foreign economic sphere. A Brookings group conducting interviews in Moscow in 1987 developed a clear sense of the relative weakness of the interest of various financial institutions in joint ventures, except as foreign currency earners. But as one looked not at institutional interests, but at the personal interests of the forty-year-olds sitting on the other side of the table, things appeared different. Can these young men, who know that they have a knowledge about foreign markets and international finance that is rare but suddenly prized in their society, really not be thinking that this is a ticket to position and even wealth over the next ten to fifteen years if the reform succeeds, and if the Soviet Union becomes deeply involved in international trade, with large amounts of foreign investment? A young Eastern European official in his country's Ministry of Foreign Trade told an American that the ministry was declining and that "I am working myself out of a job." But he added without a sense of regret, "I don't know what I'm working myself into." His Soviet counterparts must see themselves as heads of cooperative banks and trading companies, and this surely will affect their present attitudes and policy advice in a powerful way.

The same is true of the young managers in the domestic economic sphere. They may be afraid of the export market, but they hear the general secretary saying repeatedly that he is determined to push forward on reform. Young managers, like foreign economic specialists in their forties and early fifties, have to conclude that foreign marketing skills will be crucial in the economy in five years. Indeed, one of the purposes of Gorbachev's absolutely insistent language of reform must be to convince younger managers that they must bet on reform and train for its success.

There is also a broader consideration at work. In a society in which foreign travel has been a prized and restricted privilege, foreign sales and joint ventures are the guaranteed ticket abroad. The need to meet more professional standards in quality of production will be a small price to pay for acquiring the right to travel, and only someone who takes this noneconomic incentive for granted will underestimate it.

There are also issues of status. One Soviet official has noted that the joint venture law has become as fashionable as corn was under Khrushchev.[29] The analogy was not a kind one—and was not meant to be—but the word *fashionable* was an important one. A Soviet factory or cooperative manager who is not traveling abroad seeking foreign partners and foreign sales, and who does not have a foreign currency account, will almost surely lose status among his peers. Foreign currency—and the things that it can buy, such as foreign toilet paper in the factory restrooms—will become as fashionable for the fifty-year-old manager as blue jeans were for him when he was twenty. A 1987 *Izvestiia* article, "How to Earn Foreign Currency," directly appealed to managers of small plants to seek foreign partners, ending with the proper Ministry of Foreign Trade telephone number to call.[30] It is likely to become increasingly busy.

In the third place, the Soviet leadership has a clear interest in pushing economic reform. To be sure, it has been cautious in public discussions introducing it, but Gorbachev himself has recognized that foreign competition is "particularly important." The fact that the joint venture law appeared without prior discussion displays an awareness of the political sensitivity of the opening to the world economy, and the United States should entertain the possibility that—particularly at the time of a stock market crash in the West—Soviet leaders are still being less than open about their intentions.

Certainly one thing is known: the Soviet Union will never begin approaching world levels of technological sophistication until it attacks protectionism boldly. The general secretary has been extraordinarily insistent in his endorsement of radical reform and technological transformation, and he has strongly hinted at his understanding of the importance of protectionism. If he is determined to be another Peter the Great, and I think he is, he will attack protectionism head on.

29. A. Dobrovol'sky, "Za rubezhom–na khozraschete," *Lit. gaz.*, September 9, 1987.

30. "Kak zarabotat' valiutu," *Izvestiia*, September 19, 1987.

5

Choices for the United States

AMERICAN economic relations with Russia have been problematic for a century. The United States denied most-favored-nation status to the tsarist regime because of its policies toward Jews. American firms had a major role in selling the Soviet Union industrial equipment in the late 1920s and early 1930s, but Stalin halted grain exports after the famine of 1932–33, and his purchase of machinery ended with this loss of his main source of foreign currency. The period of the cold war added formal restrictions to those imposed by financial factors. The United States prohibited exports of high technology to the Soviet Union and prevented the importation of many goods (for example, crab) on the ground that they were produced by slave labor and were, therefore, unfair competition.

During the 1960s and 1970s the Soviet leadership became more interested in trade, and the increases in energy and gold prices gave it the hard currency to purchase more abroad. American restrictions were relaxed somewhat, but most of the old questions remained. At what level of technological sophistication should the exportation of machinery and the like be forbidden? To what extent should the kind of subsidized or guaranteed credit often found in international trade be extended to the Soviet Union? Should the Soviet Union be granted most- favored-nation status? As in the prerevolutionary period, the issue of Soviet treatment of its Jews became a crucial question, but now it was emigration policy rather than domestic policy that lay at the heart of the dispute.

During the 1970s, however, there was something artificial in American policy on economic relations with the Soviet Union. The U.S. Congress officially linked most-favored-nation status and subsidized credit with emigration, and the United States withheld both on the ground of unsatisfactory Soviet performance. Yet the Soviet Union for its part linked the fluctuating level of emigration not with American trade policy, but with progress or the lack of it in the strategic nuclear realm. The ups and downs of emigration coincided almost perfectly with the ups and downs in the strategic arms limitations talks (SALT I and SALT II).

In addition, arguments made by both sides of the issue in the American debates seemed all out of proportion to the reality of the time. By the mid-1980s the Soviet economy had moved past the $2 trillion level, but many wrote as if a few million dollars' worth of equipment would either raise the Soviet military threat to unseen levels or else make the Soviet Union and the United States such central trading partners that major political consequences must ensue.

In fact, the Soviet Union was importing only 15.7 billion rubles' worth of goods from the developed capitalist world by 1980 (up from 2.5 billion in 1970).[1] Since imports were constrained by export earnings and since the Soviet leaders had no intention of incurring a large foreign debt, there were real limits to how much equipment could be bought abroad. Soviet leaders had no interest in becoming too dependent on any one foreign partner, let alone its major adversary, and the foreign currency allocated to the American account went principally for feed grain. As a consequence, the Soviet Union was going to buy relatively few American manufactured goods, regardless of American policy.

Soviet purchases of manufactured goods—and of factories—from Western Europe were more substantial, and much of the American effort in its foreign economic policy toward

1. Ministerstvo vneshnei torgovli, *Vneshniaia torgovlia SSSR v 1981 g.: statisticheskii sbornik* (Moscow: "Finansy i statistika," 1982), p. 8; and *Vneshniaia torgovlia za 1971*, p. 10.

the Soviet Union was devoted to a largely unsuccessful effort to control allied trade. In the real world, the United States tended to be—or had to be—tolerant of its allies' behavior, and it "exchanged" this tolerance for allied fealty on geo-strategic and arms control questions. And, in the real world, it paid little for its tolerance. Despite the Soviet importation of foreign technology, the rate of Soviet economic growth fell from 5.0 percent in the late 1960s to 3.0 percent in the early 1970s and 2.3 percent in the late 1970s.[2]

In the next decade, however, the choices for America are going to be different from those in the 1970s. If the Soviet Union accepts foreign investment, then theoretically at least it can develop vastly expanded foreign economic relations without increasing its foreign debt, and it is easily capable of expanding its debt as well. At the same time, American choices will also be much more difficult, for joint ventures and joint production involve especially intimate types of technological cooperation. The old trade-offs between military and economic policy within NATO will be much more complicated if Gorbachev reduces the conventional threat to Europe—and he must do so if he wants radical reform. Whatever choices the United States has, there is one question on which no choice exists: Americans must think through the new situation seriously.

Choices for Businessmen

As American businessmen consider the new joint venture and joint production opportunities in the Soviet Union, they must make several different calculations. Perhaps most important of all, they must decide whether American export controls, both present and potential, make the joint enterprise possible in the short run and reasonably secure and harass-

2. Central Intelligence Agency, *Handbook of Economic Statistics, 1986: A Reference Aid,* CPAS 86–10002 (Directorate of Intelligence, September 1986), p. 64.

ment-free over the long haul. Further, they must weigh the economic opportunities and risks and the political hazards inside the Soviet Union.

The issue of American export controls is covered in the next section, and I assume for the moment that businessmen need not worry about this. In such a situation, what are the factors that must be considered as businessmen weigh the purely business aspects of investment in the Soviet Union or joint production with Soviet enterprises?

Naturally, when Americans hear Soviet officials continually admitting their uncertainty about the details of joint ventures in the future, they surely must begin with that point themselves. Soviet officials explicitly state that they are eager to learn from the experience of the first negotiations and the first joint ventures, and they are frank in saying that they will make adjustments. Like China, the Soviet Union will probably at first accept contract provisions suggested by more sophisticated western firms and later conclude that they are inequitable. Even if their conclusions are wrong, Soviet officials will be tempted to introduce modifications to restore "fairness." But by the same token they may also make modifications that remove irritants.

The first fear of a foreigner is likely to be that at some time in the future the Soviet leadership will decide to nationalize the foreign enterprises, probably with little or no compensation. Such fears, however, seem misplaced. Those in top Soviet economic circles appear to have understood the need for an attack on protectionism, and any worker resistance can easily be overcome by high enough wages or bonuses. It is easy to imagine that the joint venture program will progress slowly, because of either Soviet or foreign caution, but a xenophobic return to real isolation seems almost impossible. Autarky was an economic failure, and reinstituting it would concede that Russia will always remain backward.

Indeed, my own view is that Soviet determination to make the joint venture program a success is so strong that the first joint ventures will be virtually ensured a profit. The greater danger for a western corporation is that the Soviet Union will have an unrealistic sense of the profit level that will be required for a corporation that can receive an absolutely guaranteed 9.5 percent return on its money by investing in thirty-year treasury bonds. More daunting than the possibility of nationalization may be concerns that a joint venture in the Soviet Union will absorb a good deal of managerial energy and that the ultimate return will not be worth the effort.

American business executives will also face a series of practical concerns and questions in deciding whether to enter into joint production or joint venture agreements with the Soviet Union.

One group of concerns revolves around the operation of a joint venture in the Soviet Union. Will the multiplicity of bureaucratic institutions with which one must deal eventually produce a maddening crescendo of frustration? Will Soviet laws and paranoia about secrecy interfere with steps needed to correct problems? With a Soviet chairman of the board and managerial director, will the American minority partner continually find itself being forced into decisions that it does not favor? Will the American partner be able to select Soviet specialists and workers it admires and then retain them? Will it be forced to accept the shipment of production that it considers inferior, even for export under its brand name? Will the joint venture have the flexibility to increase and decrease production—or to change the item being pro-duced—to correspond with changing patterns of demand?

A second group of concerns centers on profitability. When the western partner is providing the patents and the equip-ment and the Soviet ·Union is providing the land and the building, the value of the relative contribution will be difficult to measure. Once the enterprise in constructed, profitability will depend, first of all, on the dollar price of labor and supplies purchased in the Soviet Union and on the price of production shipped to Soviet customers. Since the ruble is nonconvertible and prices are administered in the Soviet Union, these prices will have to be specified in long-term contracts or will have to depend on the good will of the Soviet authorities at the time they are undertaking a price reform.

In addition, the annual return will depend on many subtle factors. A slow negotiating process, with unknown results, creates initial costs that may discourage many entrants and that eventually will have to be incorporated into base costs. Slow construction or a slow subsequent decision process not only delays a return but reduces it unless profits are increased to compensate. Managerial time and effort that must be devoted to cutting through endless bureaucratic red tape is not only frustrating but costly.

Probably the most worrisome question for westerners is the repatriation of profits. The law on joint ventures states that the joint venture must be self-financing in foreign currency. That is, the amount of foreign currency expended on supplies and on repatriated profits must equal the foreign currency earned on sales abroad. For westerners the main attraction of investment in the Soviet Union is access to the huge Soviet market, but if profits earned from the domestic market cannot be exported, there is little to be gained from this access.

The problem becomes particularly difficult if the joint venture is liquidated, as is authorized under the law. Even leaving aside the possibility of dissatisfaction on the part of the westerner, American corporations merge or change their product lines frequently, and in the process they may, for typical business reasons, change their attitude toward any venture. In such cases the buyout price may be difficult to establish in an equitable way. Real "profit" in the American economy frequently is not that recorded on the operating balance sheet, but the capital gains received later when a successful enterprise (or a depreciated enterprise) is sold. If the dissolution of a joint venture simply involves the return of the original investment (let alone the depreciated value of it, as the law seems to imply), then the American partner is being cheated if the enterprise is successful and has been growing. But if the liquidation price is the "fair" market value of the enterprise and is paid in dollars, then the American partner can use dissolution as the mechanism to repatriate large scale "domestic profits" from the Soviet Union and will be tempted to do so.

With all these real and potential problems (plus the political ones at home), why should western firms become involved in joint ventures with the Soviet Union? If it is considered profitable to cooperate with the Soviet Union, licensing arrangements are a relatively simple way either to let the Soviet Union use a western invention or to pay the Soviet Union for the use of a Soviet invention. Why should western-ers go beyond licensing arrangements and accept all the complications of working with an unfamiliar bureaucracy and with officials who do not understand the norms of western business?

Obviously many businesses in the United States will decide not to become involved with the Soviet Union. Many that do will (and should) look first at licensing arrangements. Never-theless, there are a number of reasons that western firms will decide to go beyond licensing agreements to consider joint production or a joint venture. First, of course, the western firm may see the possibility of greater profit from joint ventures than from licensing arrangements. Modern multi-national firms often build plants in the third world or in the industrializing Pacific Basin countries and then import var-ious components from whichever country can produce them most profitably. Workers in developing countries such as Mexico and Taiwan are able to produce components or finished products of sufficient quality for the American mar-ket; Soviet workers should be capable of the same output under proper management and with proper machinery.

The only question is the price charged for labor and raw materials—that is, in the real world the de facto exchange rate that is established between the ruble and foreign currencies. If the Soviet Union is determined to use joint activities to acquire foreign marketing expertise, western managerial skills, and competition for its domestic manufacturers, it has every interest in setting prices at a level that gives the western firms the necessary incentive to participate. Third world countries sometimes include explicit training clauses in their contracts, and the Soviet Union may follow this path and then push the export of Soviet-produced components or feeder supplies for the western plants of their partners as the most reliable form of foreign earnings.

Second, some western firms may find joint ventures profitable because of the economies of scale made possible by the huge domestic Soviet market. For example, the Italian firm FATA is considering a joint venture in the Soviet Union to produce industrial refrigerators, calculating that a major guaranteed Soviet market will permit the construction of a larger plant than could be justified on the European market alone and that the per unit costs will be low enough to make the product profitable in the European market.

Third, western firms may fear or may actually find that their normal sales to the Soviet Union are informally linked to their willingness to participate in joint production or joint ventures. The corporation may make the decision that a low-profit joint activity will be necessary to obtain the profits from sales and that the latter compensate for the difficulties in the former.

Fourth, and probably most important, a western firm may decide to make a bet (or a hedge) for the future. If, as some suggest, the Soviet integration into the world economy in the year 2000 will not have reached the Chinese level of the early 1980s, then it is unlikely that investment in the Soviet Union will have any particular advantage over investment elsewhere in the world. A few firms may make significant profits, most will make minor profits, but the impact on per share earnings of a major corporation will probably be insignificant, regardless of whether there is a profit or a loss.

If, however, the Soviet reintegration into the world economy is a serious process that goes forward with some speed, then the calculation will be different, and significant profits may become available under various Soviet programs. In such a scenario, it is likely that in time wholly owned foreign enterprises, as well as joint ventures, will be permitted. It is probable that the Soviet Union will move toward a convertible ruble over the next decade. It is virtually certain that the Soviet Union will become at least somewhat more flexible on the repatriation of domestic profits. And it is at least thinkable that over the next quarter century the Soviet economy will undergo a genuinely radical change.

Just as the Soviet Union is looking at joint ventures primarily as a training tool at the beginning, so may many western firms make the same judgment. They will decide that they need to build up corporate expertise on the Soviet system and contacts within the Soviet system in case these become important in the future. They may decide that the early entrants may be favored when more profitable arrangements can be negotiated later.

Finally, of course, the maximization of profit may not be the only consideration for business executives. German and Japanese firms will make decisions in part in response to government pressure or government guaranteed loans, and the Soviet Union has policies it can adopt to affect the government judgments. American firms, too, live in a political environment, and it is unclear what considerations will drive the American government in the 1990s.

But noneconomic factors extend well beyond political pressures. Especially since joint activity with the Soviet Union is not likely to be associated with either large profits or large losses for major corporations in the near or even medium future, American executives will find themselves, consciously or unconsciously, being motivated by other considerations. One executive may think that technology transfer to the Soviet Union and cooperation with communist efforts to improve its economic performance is against American national interests; another may be convinced that the presence of American capitalists on Soviet soil will undercut Soviet propaganda about capitalism and will further a Soviet evolution in a market direction. One may distrust Russians, especially communist Russians; another may find relationships with them warm. One may deeply want to avoid the inevitable frustrations of dealing with the Soviet bureaucracy; another may be fascinated by Gorbachev's plans and will be eager to accept the difficulties in order to observe the economic reform unfold from an insider's vantage point. Only in some abstract economic theories are such factors unimportant. Indeed, they should be important, particularly in dealings with the Soviet Union over the next five to ten years.

Societal and Government Choices

The 1970s were featured by serious debates in the United States about the impact of economic collaboration on Soviet internal development, on the desirability of linking human rights and trade, and on the degree of restrictions to be applied. For all their intensity, however, these debates involved a considerable amount of posturing. It was clear that Leonid Brezhnev was not going to change his domestic policy very much or buy large amounts of American technology, whatever the United States did or did not do.

Similarly, despite all our talk about a growing Soviet threat—about external Soviet expansionism in the face of internal decline—overall Soviet expansionist tendencies were actually declining in the late 1970s and early 1980s, along with the decline in Brezhnev's health. By the same token, Brezhnev was never going to be particularly forthcoming in reducing armaments or in opening the Soviet Union to the West, regardless of what we did. We could posture, we could talk tough, or we could sidestep difficult decisions on arms control, precisely because there were few real opportunities being lost and little real possibility that the situation would become dangerous. While the debates about American and allied technology transfer were emotional, we knew that the technology would not be used to maximum effect so long as Brezhnev did not undertake any reform. If our allies contravened our attempts at a technology embargo or if we undercut Soviet-American trade with a Jackson-Vanik amendment, it did not matter all that much in the real world.

With the Gorbachev era, however, the choices are becoming much more real and important. It is now quite possible that Gorbachev will implement rather drastic reforms in domestic and foreign policy and that these reforms may lead to a level of joint production or joint ventures with the West that has a real impact. An effective western embargo might conceivably affect Soviet reconstruction significantly, but it might also cause the West to miss real opportunities to improve the international scene. A wooden American policy might even set the stage for the kind of Soviet foreign policy victories that were unthinkable in the Brezhnev years.

The choices, therefore, are much more difficult for the United States. First, human rights linkage will be more complex. Brezhnev was willing to permit the emigration of specific ethnic groups in exchange for certain foreign policy concessions, but he clearly would have refused to expand significantly the human rights of people who remained in the Soviet Union. Not unreasonably, the United States concentrated on the only area of human rights we could affect. Now, however, Gorbachev will be extending a series of human rights inside the Soviet Union and indirectly in Eastern Europe, some more and some less, but he may well be less forthcoming on emigration itself than Brezhnev was.

Gorbachev's human rights policy creates many dilemmas for the United States, since the United States contains many different ethnic groups that come from the Soviet Union and Eastern Europe. If we define "human rights" as emigration for only one group and thereby complicate a Soviet reform that will provide greater cultural and economic autonomy for

Ukrainians, the various Baltic peoples, Hungarians, Poles, Jews, and so forth inside the Soviet Union, we run the risk of creating resentments and antagonisms that we would be well advised to avoid.

But if the United States defines human rights more broadly than emigration, measuring progress becomes extremely difficult. One can argue whether 5,000 or 10,000 or 50,000 émigrés are sufficient for this or that American response, but at least emigration is quantifiable. How does one weigh the right of Latvians and Ukrainians to have private restaurants and shops with national dishes and goods, as well as to be somewhat freer in writing their history, when their ability to discuss the incorporation of the Baltic States in 1940 or the famine of 1932–33 remains restricted? What does one say about the legalization of the teaching of Hebrew when a few Hebrew teachers are arrested on the ground that they have become extremely active on emigration questions? How do we react to an expansion of freedom or a maintenance of restrictions on freedom in various Eastern European countries when we know that both the Hungarian reforms and the level of repression in Romania went further than Brezhnev wanted, and when we may find it hard to determine Gorbachev's influence as well?

The second reason that the choices will be more difficult for the United States is that joint production and joint ventures involve a qualitatively different level of technology transfer than outright sales of advanced products. A scholar in Soviet Georgia made the point when he stated that the purchase of a sophisticated item moves technology forward by one and one-half to two years, while the acquisition of factories and the like does so by five years, and the use of licensing arrangements by seven to eight years.[3] For this reason the United States has been loathe in the past to approve the sale of entire industrial enterprises to the Soviet Union. Even the

3. *Zaria vostoka,* May 14, 1986.

proposal to purchase a Levi-Strauss jeans factory is said to have run into difficulty because of the automatic controls that were used in its production process.

Joint production and especially joint ventures have the potential for much greater impact. The foreign partner will be providing foreign marketing techniques and training; it will be informally training managers for other Soviet enterprises; it will be bringing Soviet managers and engineers to see and learn from the home plant and its techniques; it will be serving as a powerful pressure group to improve the performance of supplier plants inside the Soviet Union; and it will have the self-interest to keep upgrading technology and production to maintain profitability.

Moreover, Soviet policy in the Brezhnev era limited the amount that could be imported, let alone used effectively. When foreign investment is being encouraged, however, there are theoretically no limits to the amount, and it may have a much greater influence at a time of major economic reform. Furthermore, some Soviet economists at least are thinking of a substantial increase in Soviet foreign debt once the reform to use it effectively is in place.

For these reasons, the debates about technology transfer will become more serious and emotional if Gorbachev is really determined to pursue his foreign economic policy. Not only will the decisions on export controls be more difficult, but longer range questions will have to be faced. A corporation will be cautious about investment in the Soviet Union if the upgrading of technology and production is likely to involve a yearly battle on export controls with a Commerce Department whose decisions reflect a desire to reward or punish the Soviet Union on current foreign policy questions.

A Policy for Americans

As we Americans begin sorting out our choices, we must, I think, face a series of fundamental questions.

First, how fragile is the Soviet Union? How effective would an embargo and a continuing military buildup be in straining and even destroying the Soviet system?

Second, to what extent would a Gorbachev reform increase the Soviet military and ideological threat, and to what extent would it simply increase pressure inside the Soviet Union to transform even further the ideology and system that we have seen as threatening?

Third, to what extent should human rights be a component of American foreign policy, especially human rights for the hundreds of millions of people who stay in the Soviet Union and Eastern Europe and do not emigrate? Would direct linkage or relaxed pressure achieve this goal best?

Fourth, to what extent does the United States have a veto over its allies in developing a coordinated policy on licensing arrangements, joint production, and joint ventures? To what extent would an attempt to enforce a coordinated policy against joint ventures and joint production disrupt the alliance?

In dealing with these issues, Americans usually wrestle with the first three questions and then assume that the allies should go along with whatever policy evolves. It seems to me, conversely, that we must begin with the fourth question. The United States produces approximately 38 percent of the GNP of the noncommunist world,[4] and by itself does not have the ability to impose an effective embargo on the Soviet Union. If politics is the art of the possible, an effective policy must take capabilities into account.

Over the last few years American capabilities vis-à-vis its allies have been at the center, though perhaps implicitly, of a fundamental debate among American specialists on the Soviet Union and American foreign policy. Most specialists have argued that Gorbachev desperately needs a nuclear

4. Calculated from CIA, *Handbook of Economic Statistics, 1986*, pp. 34–35.

agreement with the United States to strengthen his political position at home and to deal with American allies.

The unspoken implication of this argument—and sometimes spokesmen of the Reagan administration have been explicit, especially in off-the-record briefings—is that Gorbachev is in a weak bargaining position and that he will have to make concessions on arms control or emigration in order to conduct his reform. The moderates in the foreign policy and Sovietological community who hold this view have argued that we should accept such concessions; hard-liners in the administration feel that we should avoid any agreement and try to complicate the Soviet reform as much as possible.

The opposing position, with which I have been associated, is that Gorbachev has been in a strong position politically and that, if anything, a forthcoming posture toward the United States would tend to weaken him at home. (The issue of an agreement on intermediate missiles in Europe has always been a special case because it is Europe centered and can be interpreted at home as an American retreat from the Continent.) To say that radical change is possible because the adversary can be trusted is as politically difficult in the Soviet Union as it would be in the United States. The political argument for reform has always been the existence of a challenge or even a danger. Openings to Europe and Japan are easier to justify domestically than an opening to the United States.

In addition, the Soviet Union has to suspect, rightly or wrongly, that the level of American concern about technology transfer and the political difficulty of removing the Jackson-Vanik and Stevenson amendments on trade mean that, in any case, American firms will not be able to participate in joint production and joint ventures on any significant scale. If there is a determined American effort to maintain a technological blockade against the Soviet Union, the logical—indeed the only—Soviet response is to emphasize economic cooperation with Japan, Europe, and the industrializing third world countries.

The argument that Gorbachev needs to deal with the United States to facilitate relations with American allies is a stronger one. Certainly it was not a coincidence that the visit of East German leader Erich Honecker to West Germany in September 1987 occurred just before the meeting of Secretary of State George P. Shultz and Foreign Minister Eduard Shevardnadze to agree on a summit meeting. Nor was it a coincidence that Shevardnadze made his first visit to Argentina and Brazil by flying there from Washington after his meeting with Shultz. These were the real "concessions" Gorbachev received in exchange for giving President Reagan the summit he wanted.

Nevertheless, the American veto on allied actions is not absolute. The leading proponent of a multipolar strategy centered on Europe and Japan, Aleksandr Yakovlev, has now become the Central Committee secretary on the Politburo in charge of foreign policy.[5] If that strategy leads to important political concessions being made to American allies, heavy-handed American resistance could produce explosive resentments.

Even in the past the allies tended to follow the American leadership on geostrategic questions but to show independence in the foreign economic sphere. If Gorbachev reduces the size of his army and convinces the allies that the Soviet Union poses no serious military threat, the problem of alliance cohesion will become more severe. Indeed, the problem goes much deeper. The inevitable economic conflict and tension *within* the western world has been easier to handle because of the sense of community created by the Soviet threat. A reduction in the perception of this threat will tend to bring the intrawestern economic conflicts more to the political fore. One can argue that this is probably already occurring, and that a major battle within the alliance on economic policy toward the Soviet Union will accelerate the process.

5. For Yakovlev's views on this subject, see Jerry F. Hough, "Soviet Perspectives on European Security," *International Journal,* vol. 40 (Winter 1984–85), pp. 20–41.

The question that we need to face—and we do need to face it instead of hoping that it will go away—is, what does the United States gain by running such risks within the western economic community? What does it lose by working to avoid such risks?

In my opinion, the ratio between risk and reward heavily favors a modification of U.S. economic policy toward the Soviet Union. The costs of a change in policy seem minimal. It seems wildly optimistic to think that the Soviet system will shatter under pressure over the next five to ten years. Certainly those who hoped that Gorbachev needed good relations with the United States to maintain his political position and to push through his reforms have been deeply disappointed. Gorbachev did extremely well politically at home at a time when Soviet-American relations were terrible. Whatever the ultimate success of his reforms, it seems certain that he will have enough partial successes to maintain political stability at least well into the 1990s.

Paradoxically the very Americans who harbored hopes that the United States could stop Soviet reform altogether also seem to have the greatest fears that Gorbachev can transform the Soviet system overnight if he goes ahead with his reforms. They paint a picture of a major improvement in technology that will transform the Soviet military capacity. However, this view too seems wildly pessimistic. The technological gains will be slow. Although they will improve Soviet military performance,[6] the United States will surely have the possibility of reducing Soviet defense expenditures and changing its force posture in a less threatening direction by negotiation if we wish. Unless the West collapses econom-

6. Of course, the one place where the Soviet defense industry is unquestionably inferior to the American is in providing creature comforts for those manning its weapons and in creating gadgets that have a fascination beyond their military value. Surely the Soviet military is pushing for change in this respect, and we can at least hope that Soviet technological improvements will have a good part of their impact here rather than in militarily more dangerous ways.

ically, the Soviet Union will still be much behind it economically and technologically by the end of the century. The way
to keep the West militarily ahead of the Soviet Union is to
concentrate on solving western economic problems.

The potential gains of a change in economic policy toward
the Soviet Union seem much greater. First, any movement
toward the normalization of the Soviet dictatorship, toward
its de-ideologization, and toward an opening to the West is a
healthy and welcome development. It reduces xenophobia,
fanaticism, and fear—and not only in the Soviet Union—and
these are dangerous phenomena in a nuclear age. Workers in
foreign enterprises are often a contented "workers' aristoc-
racy," and exposure to foreign capitalists in joint ventures
will be deeply corrosive of old stereotypes. It will also be
hard for third world communists to maintain the same kind
of militancy when the evolution of their patron is providing
political ammunition for the moderates among them.

Second, the ideological challenge to the West that seems
most virulent and dangerous in the 1980s and 1990s is not old-
line communism, but right-wing religious or semireligious
fundamentalism. Left-wing extremism seems, in Walt W.
Rostow's phrase, to be the "disease of the transition,"[7] but
the European and Iranian experience suggests that right-wing
extremism is the disease of the middle stages of industrialization. We should not forget that "Nazi" was an abbreviation
of National *Socialism* and that the right-wing antiwestern
xenophobia in the third world implies isolation from the West
economically as well as in other ways. Hence a discrediting
of economic autarky has political benefits in noncommunist
contexts. If third world moderates can say that even the
Soviet Union understands the need for integration into the
world economy, this complicates the political task of both
right-wing and left-wing extremists seeking support.

Third, the United States has as strong an interest in a

7. Walt W. Rostow, *The Stages of Economic Growth* (Cambridge:
Cambridge University Press, 1960), p. 162.

reduction of military spending as the Soviet Union. Some Americans secretly—and sometimes not so secretly—hoped that the United States could "spend the Soviet Union into bankruptcy" with high military expenditures. Military weapon systems were often openly justified by the level of expenditures that would be required by the Soviet Union to meet them. As long as the present level of American military expenditures is associated with an ever-rising deficit, however, it harms the American economy as much as the Soviet economy, and perhaps more so. The United States has a vital national security and foreign policy interest in bringing its deficit under control. If the Soviet Union is willing to reduce its conventional armed forces, the United States has an opportunity that previous political leaders have worked hard to achieve. Huge armies in Europe have been a means, not an end, and it would be a terrible mistake to let them become an end in themselves when their original goal of reducing tensions has been achieved.

Fourth, human rights considerations now suggest a relaxation in American economic policy. In an age of Soviet *glasnost* and economic reform, it is anachronistic to treat the formal right of emigration as the only human right worth defending. An opening to the West and the development of more market relationships within the Soviet Union will mean more de facto autonomy for a range of non-Russian people inside the Soviet Union and Eastern Europe. It is hard to justify the construction of barriers to this process without a compelling military reason; it is bizarre to do so in the name of human rights—or, to be more specific, one human right.

Indeed, even if one retains old goals of promoting emigration and shattering the Soviet system, the old means are no longer appropriate. Japan sends more tourists abroad than the United States, even though it has half the American population, and this is an indispensable part of its export strategy. If the Soviet Union is serious about integrating into the world economy, it too must send hundreds of thousands and then millions of citizens abroad as business representatives, students, and tourists. Those who are really eager to emigrate will use this route. If the United States wishes to promote emigration, therefore, it should encourage Gorbachev's foreign economic reforms.

In practice, confrontation has not proved to be an effective tool in liberalizing communist systems, let alone forcing their collapse. Economic blockades have given communist rulers in Cuba, Nicaragua, and Poland the opportunity to blame their economic woes on American policy, and these blockades have strengthened militant, repressive leaders rather than weakened them. The prohibition of trade with Cuba has lasted for over a quarter of a century; no country has been so dependent on the U.S. market in theory, and yet Cuba has not modified its foreign policy, and domestically seems to be moving away from economic reform instead of toward it. By contrast, the United States relaxed its pressure against China before any major change had occurred in its domestic policy. This was followed, by chance or not, with a victory of the moderates over the so-called Gang of Four. China is such an enormous country that no doubt it was driven by its own internal forces, but, in general, if the United States removes the excuse for poor economic performance in countries such as Cuba, Nicaragua, and the Soviet Union, domestic pressure for domestic change has a better chance to build up.

In this respect, perhaps, the most sophisticated of all international relations theorists was Aesop. He once described a contest between the North Wind and the Sun to prove which was the more powerful. They competed to see which could force a man to take off his coat. The North Wind blew and blew, and the man clutched his coat more tightly around himself. The Sun simply came out from behind a cloud—and won, for the man took off his coat by himself.

Conclusion

With the passage from power in the Soviet Union, Western Europe, Japan, and the United States of the generation that remembers the foreign policy debates of the 1930s and the origins of World War II—the generation that was in its thirties when nuclear weapons were first exploded—we are leaving the postwar era. That era has been marked by great success in ending the historic enmities in Western Europe and in controlling Russia during its virulent political response to the early stage of industrialization.[8] However, the era has been marked by a failure to assimilate the implications of nuclear weapons for national security and foreign policy, for leaders have continued to think in World War II terms.[9] Because the precise nature of the new world is still not clear, we have the possibility of trying to define it as we try to understand it.

The first key to coping in the post-postwar period is to learn from Japan. In a nuclear age, military force is not as usable as it was in the past, and many military objectives are not as vital. The tragedy of Vietnam was that it really did not matter to the international position of the United States whether it won or lost. The tragedy of Eastern Europe is that the Soviet Union no longer needs it as a military buffer, but finds it politically dangerous at home either to keep it or let it go. The Japanese have learned that economic power is crucial in the nuclear age, and have been concentrating their resources on attacking American supremacy in the area that has been the real base of American national power. While the United States and the Soviet Union have been spending huge sums of money on preparations for another World War II, Japan has been winning World War III.

The second key to coping with the post-postwar period is to remember the great lesson learned in American domestic politics over the last ten to fifteen years: government control

8. See the very perceptive long-range analysis in Walt W. Rostow, "On Ending the Cold War," *Foreign Affairs,* vol. 65 (Spring 1987), pp. 831–51.

9. For a lengthy discussion of this problem, see the concluding chapter of Jerry F. Hough, *Russia and the West: Gorbachev and the Politics of Reform* (Simon and Schuster, forthcoming).

and regulation are not necessarily the answer to every problem, and the expenditure of government money often has little positive effect. Unfortunately, however, Americans have retained their old ideas about government intervention in foreign policy. Anxiety about nuclear war is "alleviated" by some meaningless weapons program or by arms control negotiations, regardless of content.

Moreover, if something unpleasant happens anywhere in the world, it is assumed that the U.S. government must do something, anything. Maybe it should make the symbolic gesture of sending an aircraft carrier, maybe it should ransom hostages who never should have been in Beirut in the first place, maybe it should provide covert military aid to rebels, maybe it should take more serious military action. But the most frequent demand—and action—is some kind of economic sanction. Time and time again such sanctions have accomplished nothing productive, but still the demand for government intervention arises the next time something happens.

We should seriously entertain the thought that government deregulation is often the most effective policy in foreign relations as well as in the domestic sphere. If restrictions—other than on matters with clear-cut military implications—are lifted from corporations and banks, they will not rush to make gifts to the Soviet Union or radical third world countries. Instead they will invest significant sums only if the economic return is reasonable and if the political risks are acceptable. If a foreign government acts in a dangerous or fanatic way, the private sector will shy away on its own. Moreover, since the private sector is pluralistic, its response will inevitably be graduated, with only a few people seeking economic contacts at the first signs of a political thaw, but an ever increasing number doing so as the foreign situation clarifies.

Soviet analysts have long recognized the great foreign policy power of western capital and economic institutions, although, of course, with alarm. At first they thought that third world nationalism would sweep away capitalism in order to expel foreign business, but now they have seen that Soviet policy must react to the reality of this power because of the economic benefits foreign business brings to the third world. Americans—and the right wing more than the left wing—have had far less confidence in the attraction of our economic institutions and capital. We should learn from the Soviet analysts.

Or, perhaps, it would be better to say that we should learn from our own earlier experience. There was a time when the United States assumed that the purpose of foreign policy was to promote the economic well-being of its citizens. We were proud to say that the flag should follow the dollar. Calvin Coolidge stated flatly that the business of America is business. But now the one president of the last fifty years who most admired Coolidge has been the most eager to impose ideological and technology-transfer restrictions on business. The president who has been most in favor of a reduction of government restrictions on business in general has been most in favor of increasing them in the foreign policy sphere.

There is a fierce debate in the United States about whether the Reagan revolution will outlive the Reagan administration and whether it should be extended. The best way to strengthen American national security in the post-postwar period is to reverse the Reagan revolution of deficit-financed military spending but to extend the Reagan revolution of deregulation into foreign policy. A good rallying cry for a new generation that wants to break with past foreign policy mistakes could be "Back to Calvin Coolidge."

OPENING UP THE SOVIET ECONOMY

JERRY F. HOUGH

Everyone familiar with the Soviet economic system recognizes its closed, completely protected, nature. The Soviet Union permits no foreign investment, imports goods only through a monopolistic ministry of foreign trade, and has no incentive system to encourage exports—indeed does not permit its factory managers to trade independently. Western countries have so long taken Soviet protectionism for granted that little thought has been given to the international implications of Gorbachev's plans to introduce domestic and foreign competition into the Soviet economy.

Soviet specialist Jerry Hough offers a preliminary assessment of the foreign policy implications of Mikhail Gorbachev's recent program of economic reform. He addresses Gorbachev's overall economic strategy and the domestic political strategy necessary to accomplish that reform, and his foreign economic policy and the related foreign policy steps he must take to implement it.

Hough sees the introduction of domestic and foreign competitiveness into the Soviet economy as an issue of major significance to the United States. He argues that the United States and its western allies have to decide now whether to try to encourage competitiveness or retard it, whether we have the power to affect Gorbachev's options, and the extent to which we can make our cooperation conditional.

In *Opening Up the Soviet Economy* Hough provides an analysis of the interplay of Soviet economic reform and foreign policy and gives policymakers information and insights needed to decide how best to respond.

Jerry F. Hough is director of the Center on East-West Trade, Investment, and Communications and a James B. Duke professor of political science and public policy studies at Duke University and an associated staff member at Brookings. He is the author of *Soviet Leadership in Transition* (1980), *The Polish Crisis: American Policy Options* (1982), and *The Struggle for the Third World: Soviet Debates and American Options* (1986).

Jacket design by Studio Grafik

The Brookings Institution
Washington, D.C.

ISBN 0-8157-3747-5